TILL THE DAY DAWNS

Till the Day Dawns

Lance Lambert

KINGSWAY PUBLICATIONS

EASTBOURNE

ISBN 0 86065 205 X

Unless otherwise indicated Scripture quotations are from
the New International Version,
© New York International Bible Society 1978.

AV = Authorized Version
crown copyright

NASB = New American Standard Bible
© The Lockman Foundation 1960, 1962,
1963, 1968, 1971, 1972, 1973

RV = Revised Version

Cover photo: Tony Stone Photolibrary—London

Printed in Great Britain for
KINGSWAY PUBLICATIONS LTD
Lottbridge Drove, Eastbourne, E. Sussex BN23 6NT by
Richard Clay (The Chaucer Press) Ltd, Bungay, Suffolk.
Typeset by Memo Typography Ltd, Nicosia, Cyprus.

Contents

Preface
Acknowledgements
1. As a thief in the night 11
2. Men spoke from God 18
3. The living and enduring word of God 26
4. The word of prophecy made more sure 34
5. According to his eternal purpose 46
6. I am the Alpha and the Omega 62
7. The times of the Gentiles 79
8. A land born in one day 97
9. The parable of the fig-tree 107
10. The great shaking 121
11. The man of sin 133
12. The coming of the Son of Man 150
13. So you also must be ready 163
14. Watch 177

Preface

This book concerns the relevance of biblical prophecy and is based on a series of messages which I have given at various times and in various places in Britain, the USA and Israel. On a number of occasions different friends have asked me to put it down in writing, and my publishers were the ones who finally persuaded me.

For those who know the Lord Jesus one of the most striking titles given to him in the Bible is 'the Daystar'. On many occasions I have seen the morning star with its brilliant light, shining above the mountains of Judea like some huge celestial lamp. It shines in the darkest part of the night and heralds the coming dawn. For the redeemed there is also a coming dawn, filled with the promise of God. Throughout the dark millennia of man's night the Lord Jesus, as the Daystar, has been the sign and harbinger of that day. The darkest part of the night, however, is still ahead, before God's day arrives and he appears to take his own. For the murkiness of that time, a promise has been given; the Lord Jesus as the Daystar will arise, with new power in the hearts of his people, heralding the day of God, and causing them to look up in joy. Their redemption is drawing near.

I consider, therefore, the subject of biblical prophecy to be of vital and strategic importance for God's people in these days. My prayer is that this book may help in our understanding of it. We have been given the word of prophecy, shining as a lamp in a dark place, until that day dawns and the daystar arises in our hearts. We would do well to pay careful attention to it, for we ignore it at our peril. If we heed it, it will lead us to his overcoming grace and power.

Acknowledgements

It is with gratitude that I acknowledge the help I have received in the writing of this book: I would like to thank Shirley Harrison of the United States who did the initial hard work in reducing the spoken messages to a written form; Alison Bartlett and Flo Dobbie of Jerusalem, Ian Macaulay and Richard Gordon of Britain, who corrected the manuscript and made many suggestions, helpful and otherwise! Margaret Bentley of Britain, Kathy Oswald and Joan Mues of the United States, who cared for the household and proved an unfailing source of help in every way; Joyce Bentley, Lily Pereboom and Meri Jones who typed the manuscript at its various stages. And last but not least, those who prayed for the work from its beginning to its end.

1. As a thief in the night

There are few subjects more vitally important for the days in which we live than that of biblical prophecy. It would not be over-stating the case to suggest that an understanding of this subject is a necessity if we are to be practically involved in attaining God's goals in the last days. So it comes as no surprise to discover that it is a subject plagued by confusion and controversy, and discredited by excess. That is exactly how we would expect the powers of darkness to operate in order to paralyse and debilitate the people of God, so divorcing them from any effective participation in the outworking of God's purpose for each phase of the end time.

Writing about the Lord's return, the apostle Paul reminded the Thessalonians: 'But ye, brethren, are not in darkness, that that day should overtake you as a thief' (1 Thessalonians 5:4 AV). The very words he used eloquently express the need to be awake, alert and realistic in our approach to this whole matter. They warn us against the possibility of being taken unawares by the coming of the Lord, and consequently suffering some kind of loss. When thieves have a burglary in mind, they give no forewarning of the time of their coming. They do not make appointments with their victims; they come unexpectedly and stealthily.

I well remember an occasion when I was a boy in my early teens, and my mother and stepfather were away, leaving an aunt to care for us. At about 2.30 a.m. she burst into my bedroom in great excitement: 'Get up quickly, Lance,' she cried, 'the whole road is alive with policemen and their dogs! We are trying to work out which of the neighbours has been burgled. I wonder whether they will catch the thief?' I leapt out of bed and followed her into the front bedroom, where my sister and my aunt were leaning out of the window, trying to ascertain which of the neighbours was the unfortunate victim. The whole avenue appeared to be full of policemen with torches and dogs, moving quietly in and out of the various gardens. After watching the proceedings for some time my aunt became thirsty, and said, 'I think I'll go downstairs and make myself a cup of coffee.' Within a few moments of her departure we were electrified by a scream that ought to have raised the dead in the parish graveyard across the river. My aunt, white-faced and shaking, was on the landing faster than it would have taken a space rocket to get there. 'He's in our kitchen!' she gasped, 'eating one of our blancmanges! He just looked at me and said "Good evening"!'

The thief, a famous cat burglar, who had that night burgled thirteen houses in our area, calmly went out the way he had entered, and disappeared into the night. On that occasion he was not caught. We had been taken completely unawares by the thief. In fact, we were so unsuspecting and so unaware of his coming that we had been seeking to determine which neighbour had been burgled, when he was actually in our own home! One cannot help but wonder how many Christians will be 'caught out' in a similar manner by the Lord's coming.

It was the Lord Jesus himself who likened his second coming to that of 'a thief in the night', saying, 'But understand this: If the owner of the house had known at what time of night the thief was coming, he would have kept watch and would not have let his house be broken into. So you also must be ready, because the Son of Man will come at an hour when you do not expect him' (Matthew 24:43-44; compare Luke 12:39-40). And again, 'Behold, I come like a thief! Blessed is he who stays awake and keeps his clothes with him, so that he may not go naked and be shamefully exposed' (Revelation 16:15). The apostle Peter further underlined this illustration when he wrote: 'But the day of the Lord will come as a thief in the night ...' (2 Peter 3:10 AV).

Paul took it for granted that the Thessalonian Christians would understand his use of the word 'thief', saying, 'You know very well that the day of the Lord will come like a thief in the night' (1 Thessalonians 5:2). For all those who know the Lord Jesus personally, there is of course nothing about him even remotely akin to a thief! If he had not himself introduced such an illustration, and the apostles had not underlined its use, it would appear offensive and cheap. The use of this startling illustration should make all true believers take seriously and realistically the subjects of Jesus' coming and biblical prophecy.

'But you, brothers, are not in darkness so that this day should surprise you like a thief. You are all sons of the light and sons of the day ...' (1 Thessalonians 5:4-5).

It seems a contradiction in terms to think of a child of God, who is described in the New Testament as a partaker of the divine nature (2 Peter 1:4), being in darkness. Darkness has no part in God (1 John 1:5), or in the kingdom of God and therefore ought to have no part in the lives of his children. They belong to the day and not to the night, and because they are the sons of light, and of the day, they ought to walk in the light.

Yet it is clear from the word of God that it is possible for those born of God to be 'asleep in the night' and 'drunk in the night'. Sleep is a state of inertia; the sleeper is alive but inert! Some Christians are living in this condition; they are not dead but they are inert! The service they offer to God

is a sleep-walking routine, for when it comes to spiritual
realities they are unable to witness or to intercede, to
worship or to overcome. In some manner they have been
compromised by the enemies of God and, walking in
darkness, have become weary, and finally have fallen
asleep. Drunkenness is a form of escapism in which the
one who drinks to excess seeks to avoid the harsh realities
of life and circumstances; the 'drunk' is alive, but
insensible to the realities around him. Some Christians
are involved in forms of spiritual escapism, at times even
using the things of God to avoid facing up to the real issues
in their lives. All who are in such a spiritual condition
could be overtaken by the day of the Lord, as by a thief in
the night.

'And we have the word of prophecy made more sure,'
wrote the apostle Peter, 'Whereunto ye do well that ye
take heed, as unto a lamp shining in a dark place, until the
day dawn, and the day-star arise in your hearts' (2 Peter
1:19 RV). Clearly and powerfully Peter sums up the
importance of this matter, not only for those to whom he
was writing, but also for all succeeding generations. The
prophetic word is a lamp, shining in a dark and squalid
place, enabling those who belong to God to see things as
they really are; it discloses the obstacles and traps which
would hinder and ensnare them, and distinguishes the
right path from false paths.

To hear and observe some Christians, one could gain
the impression that it is unnecessary to burden oneself too
much with the matter of the Lord's coming, so long as one
is saved. Yet to ignore the lamp of biblical prophecy
shining in the murky and squalid era into which we as the
people of God are now moving would be the height of
foolishness; unaware and unprepared, we shall be overtaken by the events of the last days, and if panic then
seizes us, we shall have no one to blame but ourselves.
There is, of course, no reason why this should be so. The

Lord has made every provision necessary for those he has redeemed to be found alert, watchful and ready. Even if we have been asleep, there is at present still time to awake.

It hardly needs to be stated that there are many dangers attached to the subject of biblical prophecy. I would like to draw attention to two of them. The first is the danger of an unhealthy preoccupation with the subject and particularly with prophetic details. To take to heart the word of prophecy and to give serious attention to it is wholesome and commendable, especially since it is commanded and encouraged in God's word. There can, however, be a fascination with the subject, often amounting to an obsession, which has nothing to do with the Spirit of God. It is not spiritual, but is merely the natural tendency found in many people fascinated by anything relating to the unknown future. This is the reason why astrology, fortune telling, crystal gazing, palm reading, and many other occult practices associated with divining the future have such a hold on otherwise intelligent people.

When this fascination or obsession with the future is transferred to the realm of biblical prophecy, it results in many personal and communal tragedies. At worst, it produces movements and sects founded upon strange and erroneous interpretations of prophecy, which are often involved in 'date-fixing', mass migrations or psychological mass manipulation, and even fraudulence. At best, we discover true Christians who have become cranks or eccentrics, obsessed with 'pet' theories on prophecy. They can talk for hours upon such theories, but are unable to participate in meaningful intercession, or prayer warfare, and are seldom involved practically in the building up of the church, or of their fellow-believers. They become practised in the art of correcting other Christians according to their own prophetic opinions. Having given their blind and unquestioning loyalty to some prophetic system or scheme, they become divisive over minor and even questionable detail. They appear to be tongue-tied, however, when it comes to worshipping the Lord, and paralysed when it comes to laying down their lives for him and for others. Such a danger needs to be detected and avoided at all costs.

The second is the danger of Christian cynicism concerning biblical prophecy. This is as deadly in its consequences as is unhealthy fascination or obsession with the subject, and much more common. So many true believers have, in the course of time, become spiritual cynics over this matter. They believe that biblical prophecy has been, and is, the domain of the lunatic fringe of Christianity, and that it acts like a magnet, drawing to it the unbalanced, the wild, and the emotionally unstable. They point out that all through history there have been those Christians who have believed that the Lord Jesus would return in their lifetime and that at one stage even the apostle Paul held this expectation, though he qualified it in a later letter. They treat those who have a simple and direct faith in God's prophetic word as being in a spiritual kindergarten, and their faith as belonging to spiritual babyhood.

Sometimes this cynicism is the result of disillusionment or disappointment with those who hold unbalanced prophetic views, and whose lives are spiritually fruitless and impractical. For others, it is the consequence of being damaged or misled by certain rigid interpretations and views held in a bigoted and divisive manner. For yet others, it is the very complexity and contradictory nature of the various prophetic schools of thought which have proved too much for them. They have withdrawn, in confusion, from the whole subject.

What we need to recognize is that, no matter how this cynicism is produced, the end result is the same – the people of God are asleep and unprepared for what is about to happen around them. The events of the end will overtake them with startling suddenness, and they will not be ready. That this is a dread possibility is solemnly underlined by the repeated warnings of the Lord Jesus and the apostles, 'Therefore do not be foolish, but understand what the Lord's will is' (Ephesians 5:17).

2. Men spoke from God

It is not possible to give the proper kind of attention to the prophetic word if there is no understanding in the first place of what the word 'prophecy' signifies, and who the prophet is. The apostle Peter explained that '... prophecy never had its origin in the will of man, but men spoke from God as they were carried along by the Holy Spirit' (2 Peter 1:21). This is the key to our understanding of the matter. The prophet was not simply declaring truths on behalf of God in a detached manner: *he was speaking from God as he was moved, or carried along, by the Holy Spirit.*

Through divine enabling the prophet declared that which had come to him by divine revelation, at a time of divine choosing. He was nothing less than the spokesman of God's revelation, expressing and declaring the mind and heart of God on any given matter. That which could not be understood by natural means, nor by natural intelligence and discernment, was communicated through the prophet to the world in general, and in particular to the people of God, by the Holy Spirit. Once we understand this, we begin to recognize the tremendous scope and range of biblical prophecy.

This central fact is made clear by the Hebrew and Greek words used in the Old Testament to describe a prophet, of which two, *Hozeh* and *Roeh*, signify 'one who sees' or a 'seer' (*see* 1 Samuel 9:9, Isaiah 30:10). Here we come to the heart of the matter: essentially, a prophet is a man who 'sees the Lord'. He sees what the Lord sees, and out of that vision of the Lord he speaks; in the light of what he sees of the mind and heart of God everything else is seen and interpreted. True prophecy is thus inextricably involved with seeing the Lord.

This is illustrated for us by the prophet Isaiah; by general acclaim his prophetic ministry is considered to be one of the most profound in the Bible, and it began with a vision of the Lord (*see* Isaiah 6:1–10).

Another prophet who illustrates this truth is Elisha. At one time when his frightened servant had observed that they were surrounded by hostile forces intent on capturing them, he prayed that his servant's eyes might be opened. They were opened, and he was able to see that the whole area was full of the hosts of the Lord, protecting Elisha (*see* 2 Kings 6:8 –17). This incident reveals that Elisha overcame situations and fulfilled his ministry because he saw through outward and apparent circumstances to the Lord himself. The king of Syria, at war with the king of Israel, had taken this action against the prophet because every time he had made a move against Israel, Elisha had forestalled his plans by warning the king of Israel. Consequently, the king had begun to suspect that there were Israeli infiltrators in his inner circle of advisors. Finally he challenged them, and one of his officers told him that Elisha 'tells the king of Israel the very words you speak in your bedroom' (2 Kings 6:12). Elisha did not, however, have access to some elaborate bugging system; as he saw the Lord, the Spirit made him aware of these things, and gave him insight.

The third and most common Hebrew word used to describe a prophet, *Navi,* is more obscure in its origins (*see* Genesis 20:7, Numbers 11:29). It probably comes from a root meaning 'to announce', although some believe that it is derived from an Assyrian verb '*Nabu*', to 'call', which they prefer to understand in the passive

sense, thus meaning 'the one who is called'. Still others
believe that it comes from another Hebrew root meaning
'to bubble up' or 'to pour forth'. Whatever the origin of
this particular word, it is clear that in the Old Testament
the prophet was God's spokesman, announcing what God
had revealed to him.

It is also clear that a man who claimed to be a prophet
was a false prophet unless the Lord had personally called
him. A prophet could not be formed or 'turned out' by a
'School of Prophets': he had to be called and formed by
God himself. Teachers of the law, scribes, even teaching
Levites could be produced by human training program-
mes, but not the prophet. Wherever in history there has
been a distinct prophetic gift, it has begun with a distinct
prophetic call by God. It is also clear in the Bible that the
true prophet only spoke as he was moved, or 'carried
along' by the Holy Spirit. He neither spoke his own
thoughts, however profound, nor enunciated truths simply because they were true; he spoke only when God
moved him, and the Holy Spirit caused the word of
prophecy to 'bubble up' within him.

This aspect of prophecy is further emphasized in
another Hebrew word, *Massa*, which is used in this
connection. '*Massa*' is normally translated as the English
word 'burden', meaning a 'load', or a 'thing lifted up' (*see*
Zechariah 9:1; 12:1; Malachi 1:1). It was apparently
derived from the heavy loads or burdens which were lifted
up and placed upon the back of camels and donkeys, to be
transported to the desired destination. It graphically
describes prophecy as a divinely given burden to be
delivered to others; a heavy 'load' of revelation lifted up
and placed upon the prophet by the Lord himself.

Throughout the New Testament the commonly used
Greek word for prophet is '*Prophetes*', meaning 'one who
speaks forth'. Among the pagan Greeks, of course, the
word denoted a person who spoke forth the 'oracles of the

gods', whereas in the Bible it was used of one who spoke forth the mind of God, as he was moved by the Holy Spirit. This sums up the matter for us. Prophecy is basically the forth-telling of God's mind, rather than the foretelling of the future, as generally understood. It is the revelation and communication of the mind of God on *any* given subject, past, present or future. If we are to grasp the full significance of biblical prophecy we have to understand this point.

It is a commonly held fallacy that the prophet only predicted events to come, and that biblical prophecy is a matter of divining the future. Although the prophet certainly did predict future events, it was only one element, though undoubtedly an important one, in his prophetic ministry. When speaking about the future, he did not 'divine' it, but he announced what God had revealed to him concerning it.

A careful study of the Old Testament, moreover, will lead one to the conclusion that prophecy is concerned with the nature of past events and the history of God's people, and with their contemporary situations, as well as with the future. Sometimes God spoke through the prophets recalling some long-forgotten transgression or sin, which had a significant bearing on their contemporary condition. A whole area of prophecy has to do with the explanation of past events, and is a disclosure to the people of God of the true character and consequences of those events. It also reveals the influence of unseen spiritual forces upon their execution. No amount of natural intelligence can ascertain such facts; that knowledge can only be granted by revelation. When we give heed to this area of the prophetic word, the Lord teaches us facts about history which we could not learn from any other source.

Many times the prophets dealt with contemporary situations and conditions, as on the occasion when

Jerusalem was besieged by Sennacherib and the Assyrian army. Isaiah said to King Hezekiah:

> 'This is what the Lord says: "Do not be afraid of what you have heard ... Listen! I am going to put a spirit in him so that when he hears a certain report, he will return to his own country and there I will have him cut down with the sword" ' (Isaiah 37:6-7).

And it was fulfilled exactly as the Lord had revealed.

On another occasion, when Jerusalem was besieged by a confederation of armies and the outlook was bleak, King Jehoshaphat sought God with all the people. The Lord spoke to them through a prophet, instructing them as to the action they should take:

> 'You will not have to fight this battle. Take up your positions; stand firm and see the deliverance the Lord will give you' (2 Chronicles 20:17).

When by faith they obeyed the Lord, they experienced the absolute truth of what he had said to them.

From these and many other such occasions, we learn a great deal about the Lord and his purposes for his people, about the unseen forces of darkness and their mode of operation, and about the way we can experience the deliverance and victory of the Lord, as by faith we obey the will of God.

When it comes to the prediction of future events, as opposed to a prophetic word for current situations, we are on more familiar ground, for it is with the future that most people associate biblical prophecy. It is true that a large and important proportion of the prophetic word was, and is, concerned with events to come, for even though many of those prophecies have now been fulfilled, many others still await their fulfilment. It is not hard, therefore, to understand how the popular concept of prophecy arose.

However, biblical prophecy was never a mere forecasting of future events, but rather the forthtelling of God's mind concerning the future. There in lies the difference between the occult foretelling of things in the future, and the divine word of prophecy. First and foremost, the prophetic word has always been the declaration of God's mind concerning his goal, and how all future events, both general and particular, are related to that end. It is, in fact, over the prediction of future events that some people have problems with prophecy.

Modern critical scholars who hold liberal views of God and of the Bible cannot accept the concept of supernaturally revealed facts concerning things to come. For instance, they find incredible even the possibility that God could name a king such as Cyrus two hundred years before he was born (see Isaiah 44:28 − 45:1). They are unable to accept the miraculous or the supernatural in the Bible. They make the assumption that the course of this world, and the events of history, cannot be influenced by spiritual and invisible principalities and powers, but only by man himself. This is an untenable position for the true believer.

On the other hand, conservative and Bible-believing scholars accept that there is much predictive prophecy in the Bible, and that it has been and will be fulfilled. For example, they find no problem with the messianic prophecies and their fulfilment in the Lord Jesus, nor with the prophecies concerning the exile to Babylon and the return from it, nor with the many prophecies concerning the second coming of Christ. If there has been controversy, it has been over how much prophecy remains to be fulfilled, and how literal its fulfilment will be.

Therefore, we discover that biblical prophecy not only consists of prediction, but also of explanation, definition, correction, and encouragement. On some occasions in the Bible, for instance, the word of prophecy was used simply for explanation and clarification. In revealing what was behind a contemporary situation, the Lord would explain that it resulted from the sin of his people. In other situations he would reveal that it was caused by the design of his enemies and not the sin of his people. When such a prophetic word of knowledge is given to God's people, they are halfway to victory!

In other instances in the Bible the word of prophecy was a word of definition; the Lord would define the character of a situation so that his people might know what course of action they should take. For example, Jeremiah gave prophetic counsel to the king and the people of Jerusalem, advising them, in the name of the Lord, neither to fight, nor to resist the Babylonians, but to surrender to them. In giving such advice, his case was not helped by the fact that in a previous generation, his predecessor, Isaiah, had prophesied in an altogether different vein. Isaiah had advised the nation to trust the Lord, and to make no terms with the enemy (see Jeremiah 38:1-4, 17-23; compare Isaiah 36-39).

Thus Jeremiah appeared to the leaders of his day to be a traitor. One can appreciate how confusing it must have been to hear his message; it appeared that the Lord was contradicting himself. It was, however, a totally different situation in the days of Jeremiah. Only the Lord could have defined its changed character, and indicated the different course that he wanted his people to pursue on that occasion. Jeremiah was neither advising God's people to forsake the Lord, and put their trust in Babylon, nor suggesting that the Lord was always inflexible when he had determined on judgement. In that particular situation, the rot had spread too far, and the only solution was judgement. Therefore, the faithful people of God should not fight that judgement, but accept it. This message must have been a hard one to give; yet it was an intensely practical word for those with ears to hear God in that generation. If we consider Jeremiah to be very negative, it is well to remember that it was he who also prophesied that within seventy years the nation would return to the land, and that Jerusalem would be rebuilt (*see* Jeremiah 25:11-12; 29:10-14).

On other occasions in the Bible, the word of prophecy came as a word of correction. Having revealed that sin was the root cause of some contemporary problem or crisis, the Lord would seek to correct his people, calling upon them to humble themselves before him, and to repent, and thus experience his forgiveness and restoration. This kind of correction is of the utmost importance if the people of God are to be kept aligned with God's will, and reach his goal. The purpose of prophecy was never to destroy or to pull down as an end in itself, but always to correct, so that what was of God might be strengthened, and made effective.

On yet other occasions in the Bible, the word of prophecy was a word of encouragement. During times of much trial or conflict, or when the outlook seemed bleak and dark, God spoke to his people, comforting and strengthening them. Whether it was by the assurance of his presence in their midst, or of the victory he would give them, or of the ultimate glory of his reign, he strongly encouraged them. This encouragement, sometimes reaching sublime heights of tenderness and compassion, is one of the most powerful elements in prophetic ministry and certainly the most moving.

3. The living and enduring word of God

If the Bible is no more than fossilized ancient thought expressing in often beautiful language the ways and ideals of bygone ages but irrelevant to the needs and aspirations of modern man, it would be more realistic to study the spokesmen of contemporary philosophies and ideologies. If that is so then the words of Marx, Mao, Nietzsche or Sartre would obviously be more relevant to our generation than the words of Moses, Isaiah, Paul or even Jesus. Christians cannot blame the new generation for adopting such an outlook, when they, the custodians and supposed champions of the Bible, treat it as if it were some handsome antique chair to be lovingly preserved and revered for its age but never to be used.

If, however, the Bible is the living word of God, as it claims to be, it must be relevant for all time. Anything God has said must have meaning and significance not only for the generation to which it was first spoken but to every succeeding generation. If a word from God had relevance only for the particular generation to which it was given, the value of its inclusion in the Bible would be questionable. It is important, therefore, to remember that from the beginning God intended the word he spoke to be committed to writing and handed down to all generations.

This is the truth to which the Psalmist bore witness when he declared:

'The Lord bringeth the counsel of the nations to nought; he maketh the thoughts of the people to be of none effect. The counsel of the Lord *standeth fast for ever*, the thougts of his heart *to all generations*' (Psalm 33:10-11 RV, italics mine).

The writer to the Hebrews further underlines this truth when he writes of the 'immutability of his counsel' (Hebrews 6:17) or as it is translated in the New International Version 'the unchanging nature of his purpose'. At the heart of his counsel lies absolute and unchanging truth upon which we can totally rely. During the course of history everything else will fail or decrease in value and pass away, except 'the living and enduring word of God' as the apostle Peter described it (1 Peter 1:23).

Since the Lord has given these 'thoughts of his heart to all generations', it would be inconceivable that they could become to any degree either irrelevant or futile.

'The word of God is living and active. Sharper than any double-edged sword, it penetrates even to dividing soul and spirit, joints and marrow; it judges the thoughts and attitudes of the heart' (Hebrews 4:12).

The word of God is not dead or static; it has neither exhausted its power, nor outlived its usefulness. It is living and active. The Greek word translated 'active' in the RV, NASB, NIV, and 'powerful' in the AV is an interesting word. Literally it means 'working' and we derive our English word 'energetic' from it. Far from portraying God's word as impotent and useless, as fossilized with age, it is described as throbbing with life, energy and power.

The word of God is not only alive, it is powerfully creative. Wherever and whenever the Holy Spirit is free and living faith is present, it has dynamic impact. There is sufficient energy within God's word not only to transform what is, humanly speaking, hopeless, but also to create the impossible. By his word he can bring light out of darkness, and create substance out of nothing. The advent of the twentieth century has made no difference to this eternal fact: nothing is impossible with God. His word may have first been spoken thousands of years ago but there is still within it the same life and creative power as at the beginning. The space age has neither changed God nor inhibited the living power of his word.

'Sharper than any double-edged sword, it penetrates even to dividing soul and spirit ... it judges the thoughts and attitudes of the heart.' There is always some consequence when the living and active word of God enters the being of a man or woman. For all those who have known its powerful working in their lives and circumstances, these words contain a precise description of their experience. The Holy Spirit breathes upon God's word, and people who until that moment were heedless of either God or his word are suddenly arrested by it, convicted of sin, and saved by his grace. Through his word the alcoholic is saved, delivered from his drinking, and remade; the drug addict is born of God and the power of his addiction is broken by a superior power; broken lives, broken marriages, broken homes are made whole; empty, unhappy lives are saved from the bitterness of futility to become complete in God. By his word the God of power and purpose enters aimless lives and gives to them eternal meaning and direction. Selfish and uncaring lives are changed by the power of God's word into lives of unselfish service and love. In some cases they are changed so dramatically that those lives become a byword to all who follow them. The history of God's people is full of such stories.

Ever since the Lord first spoke the word, its life-changing power has been the continuous experience of the redeemed and will be until time has passed away, and they experience his word in even deeper ways. It is a remarkable fact that although many ages separate us from Abraham, Moses, David and Isaiah, to name a few of God's servants, we have the same experience of God's word as they had. When God spoke to them, they had to trust him implicitly, and their faith in the absolute trustworthiness of his word was evidenced in their practical obedience. Paul and Peter, and many other servants of the Lord, have had the same experience through the centuries of this age. If we belong to the elect and redeemed people of God, we are all found together in a common bond of faith and obedience.

Many of those who have been redeemed by the finished work of Christ may not have dramatic stories to tell. The principle, however, is always the same: God's word comes alive to them and they experience for themselves its truth and reality; the word of Christ comes to dwell in them richly (Colossians 3:16). Every true child of God ought to be able to speak of those occasions when the word of God has shone into the heart with fresh light and power, and some spiritual surgery has been performed by it. For when the Holy Spirit takes a scripture, sometimes well-known to the person concerned, and illuminates not only that scripture but also 'enlightens the eyes of the heart', something happens which is life-changing. It is 'the word of God … penetrating even to dividing soul and spirit … judging the thoughts and attitudes of the heart'. No one who has experienced God's word in this manner would ever describe it as either dead or irrelevant to contemporary life and needs.

The many literary works of human genius have no such power as this. It would be foolish to deny them any power, for the influence of some of them on world history must not be underrated. Examples of this would be the writings of Karl Marx and Mao Tse-tung. Both these men have powerfully influenced mankind through their writings, creating political systems which have become part of human history. Another example would be the widely recognized influence on Nazism of the writings of Friedrich Wilhelm Nietzsche. The novelist Charles Dickens provides us with a further, though different, example. It is generally considered that Dickens influenced British society more than any other writer of his day, even contributing to the enactment of some much needed reforms.

The word of God, however, is in a unique category. One has never heard, for instance, of a word of Shakespeare, Goethe or Dickens, totally transforming a human being, or effecting a lasting deliverance from some destructive bondage or addiction. The analects of Confucius, for instance, are held in high esteem for their lofty ideals and ethics by those who have studied them, but one has never heard of divine light shining through them into the human heart, and working such a change that it could only be described as a new birth. However brilliant these works may be, the word of God is different from all of them, for the simple and adequate reason that it is *God's* word. That fact places the Bible in a unique class.

In this matter, I can speak from my own experience for I grew up believing that the Bible was no more than a collection of folk tales; certainly less attractive than Kenneth Grahame's '*Wind in the Willows*', probably less relevant than Aesop's *Fables*, and definitely less reliable than Hans Christian Andersen's fairy tales. Then the day came when God shone into my heart through his word and I discovered that it was 'sharper than any double-edged sword, penetrating even to dividing soul and spirit'. It brought me into a living relationship with God through the work of the Lord Jesus, and I experienced what it means to 'have been born again ... through the living and enduring word of God' (1 Peter 1:23). From that day onward I have proved that his word is 'living and active'.

In the book of Proverbs it is written: 'there are many

devices in a man's heart, but the counsel of the Lord, that shall stand' (Proverbs 19:21 RV). The Hebrew word translated as 'devices' can also be translated as 'purposes' or 'plans'. Whether we regard this scripture individually, universally or historically, man's heart has always been full of his own devices and plans.

Consider the philosophies, ideologies and religions, that have sprung from the 'devices in a man's heart'; the great empires that have been produced by the purposes in a man's heart; the unending line of emperors, kings, presidents, tyrants, despots and dictators in whose hearts there have been such plans and devices.

Consider, too, the effects of these 'devices in a man's heart'. It is no exaggeration to claim that at times the life or death, the well-being or the enslavement, the joy or the misery of multitudes of people has been determined by such. 'The final solution of the Jewish problem' was a device in the hearts of the Nazi leaders of the 'thousand year Reich'. Their might and authority was unchallengeable in their heyday, and it appeared that their plan would succeed and their 'Reich' last for ever. In the final analysis, however, it was not Adolf Hitler's final solution of the Jewish problem which succeeded. For, in spite of the fact that more than six million Jews died in the most horrific circumstances, and millions more were maimed for life in either body or mind, it was God's final solution of the Jewish problem which succeeded. Today the state of Israel is a reality, and 'the thousand year Reich' has disappeared. There are many other examples which could be selected from history or from the contemporary world scene but it is the counsel of the Lord which outlasts them all.

Much of this world's story is condensed in some of the phrases we have considered – 'the counsel of the nations', 'the thoughts of the peoples', and 'the devices in a man's heart'. From the standpoint of time they would appear to

be the governing factors in the life and history of the
nations, for they express those values which the sages of
the day considered to be permanent, rational and relevant
to human needs and aspirations. Observed, however,
from the standpoint of the eternal, they are only dust on
the divine scales, for they are revealed as finite and
transient values, irrelevant to the genuine and abiding
needs of mankind.

In words that are majestic in their simplicity and depth,
Isaiah prophesied, saying:

> 'All men are like grass, and all their glory is like the flowers of
> the field. The grass withers and the flowers fall, because the
> breath of the Lord blows on them. Surely the people are
> grass. The grass withers and the flowers fall, but the word of
> our God stands for ever' (Isaiah 40:6-8).

However powerful and glorious men may seem, they all
pass away. The list of great names from the past is endless
– Nebuchadnezzar, Alexander, Nero, Charlemagne,
Napoleon, Hitler, Stalin, Mao. They have all come and
they have all passed away; and there are others yet to
come who will also pass away.

All these leaders have appeared on the scene strong,
vigorous, and energetic, like the winter grass of Israel
which suddenly springs up fresh and green. They come to
their full power and glory like the wild spring flowers
which bloom with such startling vividness and carpet
Israel with their beauty. But like the grass and the wild
flowers they have died, for when the time comes the hot
dry desert wind blows and however vigorous it was the
grass withers and dies; and those flowers, however stately
and beautiful they were, they too shrivel and die.

It is alway good to remember that it is 'the breath of the
Lord' which blows upon men and all their glory. He
terminates their lives, and exposes their earthly values as
transient and corruptible. The Psalmist agreed with this

truth when he declared: '*The Lord* bringeth the counsel of the nations to nought; *he* maketh the thoughts of the peoples to be of none effect' (Psalm 33:10 RV, italics mine). The real issue of time and history then appears in stark colours: in the final analysis it is neither a question of strength, authority, intelligence, fame or human beauty and glory, for when everything belonging to fallen man and his glory has disappeared, it is the word of our God which will stand for ever.

The real issue is whether the truth expressed in his word has entered into our lives saving us from futility, changing us into the likeness of the Messiah, Jesus, and training us for eternal glory and service.

4. *The word of prophecy made more sure*

The fact that at least a quarter of the Bible consists of prophecy ought to catch the attention of every faithful Christian. If it is true that the word of God as a whole has significance and meaning for all generations, the word of prophecy must surely have specific relevance too. It has been estimated that out of the Bible's 31,124 verses, 8,352 verses contain predictive material; or, to state it in another way, 27 per cent of the word of God is prophetic. This figure, of course, contains not only the many prophecies which have been fulfilled, but also those which remain to be fulfilled.

Most Christians will accept the *lessons* of prophecy. If they have problems with this subject, they are concerned with what remains to be fulfilled, and when that fulfilment will take place. They agree that prophecy is relevant to them in the sense that in times past God revealed his mind concerning many matters through his servants, even predicting events which were to come to pass. All are in agreement that from such prophecies, important lessons can be drawn relating to the character of the Lord, and to the ways in which he cared for his own and corrected them. They will even accept that a number of prophecies refer to the second coming of Christ, and will be fulfilled at some indeterminate, probably distant point in the

34

future. They believe that his return, as a part of the orthodox Christian faith and creed, should be affirmed.

The principal problem for so many concerns how much of the prophetic word remains to be fulfilled, and whether any of its fulfilment in practical terms relates to our time. This is the point on which so much of the controversy and confusion is centred. Some Christians cannot accept that God might have spoken with clear and practical implications about the days in which we live. They find it difficult to accept that a prophetic word given centuries ago requires a definite practical response, if loss is to be avoided. Nevertheless, it would seem strange if the Lord had said so much concerning the centuries from Adam to Paul and very little concerning the course of history from that time onwards, particularly as the ages reach their climax. The Bible reveals that he is the God of history, working out 'everything in conformity with the purpose of his will' (Ephesians 1:11); that 'the Most High is sovereign over the kingdoms of men and gives them to anyone he wishes' (Daniel 4:25); that 'from one man he made every nation of men, that they should inhabit the whole earth, and he determined the times set for them and the exact places where they should live' (Acts 17:26).

In this light, it would be remarkable if God had said nothing about the days in which we live, especially since the nations now possess the kind of weapons which could destroy all human life and cause the dissolution of the planet. In fact it would appear that in the words of the Lord Jesus we have an intimation that at the end precisely this kind of situation would necessitate the intervention of God. In Matthew chapter 24 verse 22 it is recorded that he predicted: 'If those days had not been cut short, no-one would survive, but for the sake of the elect those days will be shortened'. Until recent times no world situation could have fitted this description.

The Lord declares:

'I am God, and there is no other; I am God, and there is none like me. *I make known the end from the beginning, from ancient times, what is still to come.* I say: My purpose will stand, and I will do all that I please ... What I have said, that will I bring about; what I have planned, that will I do' (Isaiah 46:9-11, italics mine).

Or again he says:

'Who *foretold this long ago*, who *declared it from the distant past*? Was it not I, the Lord? And there is no God apart from me, a righteous God and a Saviour ...' (Isaiah 45:21, italics mine).

The Lord Jesus himself, speaking to his disciples concerning the events of the end, said:

'See, I have told you ahead of time' (Matthew 24:25),

and speaking about the promised Holy Spirit only hours before his arrest and crucifixion, said:

'But when he, the Spirit of truth, comes, he will guide you into all truth. He will not speak on his own; he will speak only what he hears, and *he will tell you what is yet to come*' (John 16:13, italics mine).

These statements make it transparently clear that the Lord uses prophecy to reveal the future in the light of his own purpose. It is not the only function of the word of prophecy but it is an important and strategic use of it. The Lord has a strategy for each phase of time and wishes to involve his people in its execution. In order to serve the counsel of God in our own generation, it is necessary to know his plan for it, and more than in any other way, this reveals the practical relevance of the prophetic word for those who wish to serve him. Furthermore, such an understanding of how it relates to our times and how the people of God should be involved in its outworking demands a whole-hearted and uncompromising faith and obedience. He reveals the 'end from the beginning' in order that when those events which he has predicted begin to be fulfilled, his children might know that he is God alone, and that he has control of all things, even when the opposite may appear to be true. He will not fail. He will fulfil his purpose exactly as planned and will enable those who trust him to overcome and be faithful to the end, whatever the cost entailed.

The apostle Peter wrote:

> 'And we have the word of prophecy made more sure; whereunto ye do well that ye take heed, as unto a lamp shining in a dark place, until the day dawn, and the day-star arise in your hearts' (2 Peter 1:19 RV).

He graphically describes the prophetic word as 'a lamp shining in a dark place'; nothing could be more important or relevant to a traveller trapped in murky darkness or in thick fog than a lamp giving a clear light. In those circumstances, even a map would lose the greater part of its value unless such a traveller had some form of light. The prophetic word is such a lamp. No matter how deep and murky the darkness which at times may envelop the path ahead for God's people, it has light to shed upon every step of the way. Through it the Holy Spirit is able to reveal hidden and unsuspected dangers lurking in the dark, which would otherwise waylay many, and is able to explain the true nature of worldwide situations and circumstances facing his people. Without such illumination they could be deceived. He is able by the same means to encourage them in times of great distress to look up and endure in hope, by disclosing the divine end and revealing the enthroned Messiah to the eye of faith.

We are to pay attention to the word of prophecy as to 'a lamp shining in a dark place, *until the day dawn, and the daystar arises in your hearts*'. The word of prophecy is not merely relevant until the end of the New Testament era

but until the day of the Lord's coming dawns, and the
morning star heralding that new day has arisen in the
hearts of true believers. 'And the daystar arises in your
hearts' is a striking and unusual phrase. The Lord Jesus
speaks of himself as 'the bright Morning Star' (Revelation
22:16). Its context would suggest that those who are
faithful and who have given serious attention to the
prophetic word will be granted special spiritual experi-
ences of the Lord as his coming draws near. The Spirit of
Christ will quicken them in the light of his return, giving
them understanding of their times, and equipping them to
fulfil his will and work his works.

Biblical prophecy is infinitely more relevant to this
generation than the projections of the modern mass
media; it is not only relevant, it is also reliable and
accurate. Many people of our generation will have heard
on radio or on television, or read in newspapers, magazines, or even intelligence surveys, the predictions and
interpretations of future events by expert analysts, or at
the least, their projections of future trends and their
significance, only to discover in the course of time that
they are totally inaccurate. On the other hand, biblical
prophecy has never been proved inaccurate but has been
fulfilled exactly as foretold time and again. For this reason
the apostle Peter having described the prophetic word as a
'light shining in a dark place until the day dawns ...',
wrote, 'and you will do well to pay attention to it' (2 Peter
1:19). It is effective and operative until the end of the age
and the return of the Messiah and it would be the height of
stupidity to ignore God's divinely authoritative and
inspired advice.

Peter made another striking statement when he wrote
'And we have the word of prophecy *made more sure* ...'
(italics mine). This rendering of the Greek in the Revised
Version is more accurate than the rendering in the
Authorized Version 'and we have a more sure word of

prophecy' which could suggest, as some have understood it to mean, that Peter was making a comparison between the prophecies of the Old Testament and those of the New Testament. He was, however, pointing out the fact that since a large portion of biblical prophecy had been precisely fulfilled by that time, faith in its reliability and relevance ought to be greatly strengthened. In this connection, it is both instructive and encouraging to note that out of approximately 590 major events prophesied in the Bible, all except twenty have been fulfilled. For the people of God living in the latter half of the twentieth century, the word of prophecy has been made even more sure than when Peter wrote his letter!

Certain prophetic passages in the Bible are sealed up until the time of the end and may not have any practical relevance for generations which have not entered that time. Those passages, which are not many, will not make sense until the era for which they were written arrives. When that time arrives divine wisdom will be given and they will spring into life and be understood. For instance, in Daniel chapter 12 verse 4, it is written: 'But thou, O Daniel, shut up the words, and seal the book, even to the time of the end; many shall run to and fro, and knowledge shall be increased' (AV). The thought is repeated in verses 9 and 10: 'And he said, Go thy way, Daniel: for the words are closed up and sealed till the time of the end ... and none of the wicked shall understand; but the wise shall understand' (AV).

Such prophecies will never be understood until the Holy Spirit gives special wisdom, and this point should never be overlooked. For example, it is written in Revelation 13:18, 'Here is wisdom. Let him that hath understanding count the number of the beast; for it is the number of a man: and his number is Six hundred three score and six' (AV); and a further example is found in Revelation 17:9 where it is stated, 'Here is the mind which hath wisdom. The seven heads are seven mountains, on which the woman sitteth.' There have been many attempts to identify 'the beast' and 'the woman' which may or may not be valid, but when a practical understanding becomes a necessity, the Lord will grant the necessary wisdom to those of his servants in whom he finds faithfulness and humility.

In the same category we ought to place the small but significant interjection recorded in both Matthew 24:15 and Mark 13:14: 'Let him that readeth understand.' The implication is that more than normal and natural intelligence is required if the reader would understand the meaning of that prophecy; it requires wisdom which only God is able to give.

This is an elementary principle in the believer's whole approach to the word of God, whether it is to the Bible in general, or to biblical prophecy in particular. The mastery of God's word by natural, human intelligence has always been disastrous in its consequences, for the living God is not under compulsion to give an understanding of it to anyone, nor to unveil the secrets of his heart. He demands a humble, open faith and obedience and will always grant more light on his word, when we obey the light he has already given. At times, one meets in a certain type of Christian an arrogant and impatient mentality determined to master and solve every detail of biblical prophecy and produce a 'fool proof' prophetic scheme for presentation to the Christian public. But the Lord is not honour-bound to unlock every prophetic 'riddle' before its time. So much of the erroneous or unbalanced teaching on prophecy which has afflicted the church has stemmed from this attitude.

There are some prophecies which the people of God are able to understand in human terms only in the twentieth century. Until then their fulfilment was conceived as being a dramatic and supernatural intervention of God.

There is no doubt that this will be the manner in which many of these prophecies will be fulfilled (*see* Matthew 24: 29-31; 1 Thessalonians 4:16-17).

Nevertheless, certain events are predicted and precisely described which only the child of God living in the atomic age is able to understand scientifically. For instance, the apostle Peter, formerly a fisherman and, as far as it is possible to ascertain, without any advanced education, described the day of the Lord in terms which most schoolchildren in the mid-twentieth century would identify as nuclear. He wrote:

'But the day of the Lord will come as a thief in the night: in which *the heavens shall pass away with a great noise, and the elements shall melt with fervent heat*, the earth and also the works that are therein shall be burned up. Seeing then that all these things shall be dissolved, what manner of persons ought ye to be in all holy conversation and godliness, looking for and hastening unto the coming of the day of God, wherein *the heavens being on fire shall be dissolved, and the elements shall melt with fervent heat*?' (2 Peter 3:10-12 AV, italics mine).

These words of Peter, using descriptions only too familiar to us today, were written about 1900 years ago. Anyone who has witnessed first-hand, or on documentary film, an atomic explosion can understand such terms as the heavens 'passing away with a great noise or roar'; or 'the heavens being on fire'; or 'the elements dissolving with fervent heat'; or 'the earth and its works being burned up'.

Some 400 years earlier the prophet Zechariah had also prophesied concerning the last days, when he predicted,

'And this shall be the plague wherewith the Lord will smite all the people that have fought against Jerusalem; *Their flesh shall consume away while they stand up on their feet, and their eyes shall consume away in their holes, and their tongue shall consume away in their mouth*' (Zechariah 14:12 AV, italics mine).

Zechariah has described for us accurately and vividly
the immediate after-effects of a nuclear blast, but until the
mid-twentieth century no one who read his words would
have been able to understand them in human terms. A
plague which could suddenly cause the decay or consump-
tion of the flesh, the eyes and the tongue, before people
could even change their position and run for cover, or
throw themselves down upon the ground was unimaginable until Sunday, 5th August 1945. On that day an atomic
bomb was dropped upon the Japanese city of Hiroshima
and, in less than a minute, it was incinerated and 100,000
people had died. More than a mile from the centre of the
blast, people's flesh disappeared, their eyes melted, and
their tongues dissolved, in whatever position they happened to be at the moment of the explosion.

Ezekiel prophesied concerning a war to be fought
against Israel during the last phase of world history, in
which many nations will participate, led and inspired by a
power from the far north (see Ezekiel chapters 38 and 39).
In that prophecy he employs striking terms to describe the
arrangements for the disposal of the large number of
enemy dead resulting from the intervention and judgement of God. He wrote,

> 'On that day I will give Gog a burial place in Israel ... It will
> block the way of travellers, because Gog and all his hordes
> will be buried there ... For seven months the house of Israel
> will be burying them ... Men will be regularly employed to
> cleanse the land. Some will go throughout the land and, in
> addition to them, others will bury those that remain on the
> ground. At the end of the seven months they will begin their
> search. As they go through the land and one of them sees a
> human bone, he will set up a marker beside it until the
> grave-diggers have buried it in the Valley of Hamon Gog'
> (Ezekiel 39:11-16).

If this judgement of God is to be a miraculously timed
earthquake, the manner of burying the dead, as described

in the prophecy, is highly abnormal for the following reasons.

Firstly: the risk of plague diseases following an earthquake is so high that *the* priority is to bury the dead as quickly as possible in mass graves near the scene of the disaster. According to this prophecy, the enormous number of dead are buried in a special ravine or wadi set aside for that purpose, which will be closed thereafter to travellers and visitors. It is located east of the Dead Sea in what is now the kingdom of Jordan. In commemoration of the event, it will be renamed 'the Valley of Hamon Gog' or 'the Valley of the hordes of God' (*see* Ezekiel 39:11,15).

Secondly: Israel will take seven months to bury the dead, and at the end of that period will institute a final careful search of the whole land for any bodies or bones which may have been overlooked. The length of time taken, the care with which the work is undertaken, and the final search of the land are signs which suggest that the dead are contaminated in an unusual manner (*see* Ezekiel 39:12,14).

Thirdly: special squads of workers will be organized to locate the dead bodies but not to touch them, and whenever and wherever such bodies are discovered they will set up markers for further special squads who will remove them to the reserved burial place. The biblical laws concerning the burial of the dead, and concerning defilement through contact with dead bodies, would not explain these arrangements (*see* Numbers 19:11-22). The evidence more likely suggests that the bodies are contaminated in a manner which requires specialized treatment by trained workers (*see* Ezekiel 39:14-15).

Taking these factors into consideration, it would be impossible to explain the unusual arrangements for burial if the large number of dead was caused by a natural earthquake. It is true that in Ezekiel 38:19 the Lord says,

'...surely in that day there shall be a great shaking in the
land of Israel' (AV). The Hebrew word translated in the AV
and RV as 'shaking' and as 'earthquake' in the NASB and
NIV, means noise, tumult, uproar; or shaking, quaking; or
earthquake. The same word is used in the next verse in the
phrase 'shall shake at my presence'. Whether this shaking
is due to a natural earthquake or to some other cause, it is
the Lord who commands it, and its consequences are the
same: 'the mountains shall be thrown down, and the steep
places shall fall, and every wall shall fall to the ground'
(verse 20). Comparing Ezekiel 38:19-22 and Ezekiel
39:4-6 it is possible that some form of nuclear explosion is
predicted, and it follows, therefore, that what could not
have been understood in practical terms in earlier centuries, is clear in the twentieth century – the multitude of
dead bodies described by Ezekiel could be radioactive,
which would explain the unusual arrangements for their
burial.

In the light of these truths, it is not insignificant that in
'the closing passages of the book of Revelation the Lord
Jesus declares, 'Behold, I am coming soon! Blessed is he
who keeps the words of the prophecy in this book'
(Revelation 22:7). As if to emphasize this matter, John
writes at the beginning of the book, 'Blessed is the one
who reads the words of this prophecy, and blessed are
those who hear it and take to heart what is written within
it, because the time is near'. (Revelation 1:3). There is a
specific blessing for those who read the Revelation of
John, and who, on hearing what the Spirit is saying
through it, take to heart its practical significance.

In the popular view, biblical prophecy and blessing are
not normally associated with each other. It is therefore
worth noting that a promise of particular blessing is given
to those who approach the prophetic word with a serious
and sensitive spirit. Many Christians have particular
difficulty over this book, and one is bound to note that the

difficulty has been made much more complex by the large number of books which have been written on it, presenting many and conflicting interpretations, not all of which are helpful!

One is reminded of the story of the man who sought light on the Revelation of John by studying the many books and commentaries written of it and, having wrestled with their various and contradictory interpretations, finally in desperation took some aspirins, put a pack of ice on his aching head, and returned for relief to reading the actual book of Revelation! No amount of difficulty, however, should be allowed to deter the child of God from keeping 'the words of the prophecy of this book' and from experiencing the promised blessing.

Furthermore, it is not a coincidence that as well as completing the canon of Scripture, and summing up the Bible, the Revelation of John is also the final word of biblical prophecy. Since its position is the work of the Holy Spirit, the words of the Messiah in Revelation 22:7 ought to be understood as referring not only to this book in particular, but to the whole Bible in general. If that is the case, it is clear that the Messiah considers the word of prophecy to be relevant to all generations of his people, and specifically relevant to those who will live in the last phases of world history. Shall we contradict him and ignore the prophetic word at our peril, or shall we take it to heart and discover that whatever the trials or conditions through which his people will have to pass, that word has been given to them for their security and their blessing?

5. *According to his eternal purpose*

In the preceding chapters it has been emphasized that biblical prophecy is relevant throughout time for the redeemed people of God, and holds particular significance for them during the last phase of world history. Little, however, has so far been written about the content of that relevance. The question is bound to arise in the minds of some of my readers as to how the particular subjects to be dealt with in the next two chapters relate to prophecy. The answer is that they are essential aspects of prophetic ministry and if overlooked would leave our understanding of the prophetic word seriously impaired.

One major aspect of the relevance of biblical prophecy for the child of God is that it explains the ages of time and the creation of man, and reveals the divine goal in history. It provides the key which unlocks many riddles. For what purpose were man and the universe created? What is the significance of man's unique constitution? Why is there wickedness and evil in mankind and what is its origin? What is the purpose of God's redemption? Is there any solution to the world's problems and are the nations moving towards that solution? If biblical prophecy is the revelation of God's mind concerning the nature and the end of human history, as the Bible claims it to be, then its relevance becomes immediately clear. No one could give a more authoritative and accurate explanation of it than God. All the intelligence in the world could not have discovered such truth, for he alone is able to reveal it.

The Holy Spirit used the apostle Paul to communicate this truth when, for instance, in Ephesians 3:11, he referred to '...the eternal purpose which he purposed in Christ Jesus our Lord' (RV). God had an original purpose for mankind and the universe long before sin made its entrance into history and man fell. Neither the fall of man, nor the ongoing wickedness and rebellion of the world, nor even the faithlessness and compromise of his redeemed children has deflected the Lord from that purpose. Some Christians confuse the eternal purpose of God with his plan of salvation, but although they are directly related and have become intertwined in their practical execution, in the person of the Messiah, they need to be distinguished from each other.

Although popularly understood in terms of teaching, Colossians 1:14-23 is in fact prophetic. In the preceding verses (3-14) the apostle Paul had been informing the Christians at Colosse concerning the burden of his prayer for them, and concluded with the words, 'For he has rescued us from the dominion of darkness and brought us into the kingdom of the Son he loves, in whom we have redemption, the forgiveness of sins' (verses 13-14). He then proceeds with a remarkable explanation of human history so profound and sublime that it could only have been given through divine revelation. He writes: 'He is the image of the invisible God, the firstborn over all creation. For by him all things were created: things in heaven and on earth, visible and invisible, whether thrones or powers or rulers or authorities; all things were created by him and for him. He is before all things, and in him all things hold together' (verses 15-17).

These words explain the true significance of man and of creation. Without such an explanation it would be impossible to adequately understand human history, or to discern any purpose in man and in the universe. Life would have to be relegated to the realm of confusion and coincidence in which some kind of evolutionary process might be found, but which could hold little hope for the future. An entirely different picture is painted by these words. They reveal the Messiah at the heart of God's eternal purpose for mankind and for creation.

The Lord Jesus is 'the image of the invisible God' – the manifestation and the visible representation of the Un-seen and Almighty God. He is 'the firstborn over all creation' – the first in the whole creation regarding priority and pre-eminence, with divine authority and purpose centred in his person. 'By Him all things were created ...' – he is the agent of all creation; through him, man and every created thing were made. 'All things were created ... for him' – he is the reason for all creation. 'In him all things hold together' – he is the power of the whole creation. Simply stated, this means that the Messiah is the key not only to our understanding of the divine purpose and destiny of man, but also the divine purpose for all created things, whether heavenly or earthly, unseen or seen. Without this understanding, all life appears to be a tangled mass of unrelated and broken strands in which it is impossible to recognize any design or goal.

Moved by the Holy Spirit, the apostle Paul continued,

'And he is the head of the body, the church; he is the beginning and the first-born from among the dead, so that in everything he might have supremacy. For God was pleased to have all his fulness dwell in him, and through him to reconcile to himself all things, whether things on earth or things in heaven, by making peace through his blood, shed on the cross. Once you were alienated from God and were enemies in your minds because of your evil behaviour. But now he has reconciled you by Christ's physical body through death to present you holy in his sight, without blemish and free from accusation ...' (verses 18-22).

Note carefully the phrases 'all things were created *by him* and *for him*' (verse 16); '... the Son he loves, *in whom* we have redemption, the forgiveness of sins' (verses 13,14), 'But now he has reconciled you *by Christ's* physical body through death ...' (verse 22); and '*through him* to reconcile to himself all things ... by making peace through his blood ...' (verse 20). In the person of the Messiah both the work of creation and the work of redemption are centred. The Lord has not laid aside the original design which he had when he created man and the universe but intends to fulfil it precisely as planned; and it is in its fulfilment that his plan of salvation and his eternal purpose are combined. In fact, the work of salvation, which the Lord Jesus accomplished through his death on the cross, is the means by which God re-introduces mankind to his original purpose. It is sad when believers understand only his saving work, as if that were his goal, and have little or no understanding of his eternal purpose.

'He is the head of the body, the church; he is the beginning and the firstborn from among the dead, so that in everything he might have the supremacy' (verse 18). With these words the apostle introduces the heart of God's eternal purpose: to have a people in such union with the Lord Jesus that it can only be described as the organic oneness of head and body. In this manner the Messiah is the beginning of a new man and a new day, the firstborn from among the dead. God has not only crucified the old with Christ but has also 'given us new birth into a living hope through the resurrection of Jesus Christ from the dead' (1 Peter 1:3). Furthermore, he is also the beginning of a new creation. God plans 'through him to reconcile to himself all things, whether things on earth, or things in heaven' (Colossians 1:20). In some mysterious manner the full spiritual growth of his true Church is related to the final reconciliation and liberation of the natural creation. The apostle writes:

'The creation waits in eager expectation for the sons of God
to be revealed. For the creation was subjected to frustration,
not by its own choice, but by the will of the one who subjected
it, in hope that the creation itself will be liberated from its
bondage to decay and brought into the glorious freedom of
the children of God' (Romans 8:19-21).

It is hard to imagine what the natural creation will
become when it is liberated from its bondage to decay, for
even in its present state it is at times incredibly beautiful.
The prospect should fill every child of God with joyful
anticipation of that new heaven and new earth in which
righteousness will dwell.

A charge made repeatedly against the Bible is that it
gives man a unique position in the creation, placing him at
the heart of everything, as if the universe revolves around
him. This concept is contrary to the modern view of man
as an ordinary part of the natural creation whose evolution from matter follows in principle the evolution of the
animal and vegetable world. A superficial reading of
Genesis chapter 1 and 2 would yield enough evidence to
support the view that man is unique, but when the whole
Bible is taken into consideration, the evidence becomes
overwhelming. Only God could have revealed that man
was made in his image and after his likeness (Genesis
1:26) and that, unlike the rest of the warm-blooded
creation, he breathed into man something of himself
(Genesis 2:7). These facts place man in a unique category
when compared with all other created things, for he alone
has a 'capacity' for God, and was created spirit, soul and
body, (see 1 Thessalonians 5:23 and Hebrews 4:12).

There are Christians who would dispute this truth,
considering that man was created only soul and body, and
that the spirit of a man is the higher part of his soul, or
merely another name for it. The scope of this book would
not allow an adequate handling of the subject but, in my
view, a careful reading of the Bible would lead to the

conclusion that man consists of spirit, soul and body. Whatever conclusion is reached, all true believers will accept the words of the preacher in Ecclesiastes 3:11 'He has also set eternity in the hearts of men; yet they cannot fathom what God has done from beginning to end.' Man is neither a human ape, nor even a highly intelligent and sensitive animal. He has been created in the image of God with an emptiness in his spirit which only the presence of God is able to fill. The prophetic word of God reveals that man is unique in the natural creation, and that God created all things with him in view. It declares that man was designed to obtain the glory of God and, in union with him, to rule all things. It was from this high calling that he fell and became more animal than human, and history provides the sad and ample evidence of that fact.

This truth has very great significance and relevance for the people of God in these days, for if man was not created by God in his image, then he is merely an animal, evolving from matter like all other forms of life. It then follows that when society deems it necessary, men and women could be exterminated in the same manner in which cockroaches or flies are exterminated. If circumstances were to demand the liquidation of a kind of person, or a class of people, *for the higher good*, it would be possible for a nation to undertake their destruction with as little conscience as unwanted animals are put to sleep. Concept governs behaviour. The theory and practice of abortion, euthanasia, genocide, the murder of innocent people as a means of political pressure, and the destruction of whole classes of people are based on this concept. On the other hand, if every human being, however apparently worthless, debased, or animal-like in appetite and behaviour, is conceived to be a person originally made in the image of God, a person with an eternal destiny for whom Christ died, society's entire attitude toward mankind would be of a different order. Even when the image of God is almost defaced in people, the redeeming love of God is not only able to reach and save them, but is also able to remake them and restore them to his original purpose.

Furthermore, the word of prophecy sheds light on the vexed question of abortion, for it reveals that human personality and being begins *in the womb* and not at birth. Isaiah prophesied, saying, 'This is what the Lord says – he who made you, who *formed you in the womb* ...' (Isaiah 44:2, italics mine; *see also* verse 24). Isaiah amplified this truth when he declared, 'And now the Lord says – he who *formed you in the womb to be his servant* (Isaiah 49:5, italics mine). It is further emphasized by Jeremiah when he testified, 'The word of the Lord came to me, saying, "Before I formed you in the womb I knew you, *before you were born* I set you apart ..." ' (Jeremiah 1:4-5, italics mine).

The truth is even more clearly expressed by the Psalmist when he said, 'For you created my inmost being; you knit me together in my mother's womb' (Psalm 139:13). If the prophetic word is true and the life and personality of a human being begins at conception and not at birth, it follows that abortion is murder, and there is no way in which it can be legitimized in God's sight. It is no coincidence that in Germany the Nazis commenced with the legalization of abortion, progressed to euthanasia, the 'mercy killing' of the mentally ill and unstable, and ended with genocide, the mass murder of 6,000,000 Jews and 1,500,000 gypsies.

This kind of truth is unpalatable to some Christians for it contradicts contemporary ideas and theories about human life and raises uncomfortable and disturbing issues for them. It is easier to dismiss it as old fashioned, impractical or out-dated and be identified with the popular outlook than to swim against the current. Nevertheless, it is as much the truth of God as the truth of his love, or the truth of his salvation. If it is ignored or dismissed, it will have the same serious consequences for those who are individually involved in these evils, as for the nations which legalize them.

In his letter to the Colossians, the apostle Paul wrote of 'the mystery that has been kept hidden for ages and generations, but is now disclosed to the saints' (Colossians 1:26). This is a recurring theme in Paul's writings for in his Ephesian letter he wrote, 'In reading this, then, you will be able to understand my insight into the mystery of Christ, which was not made known to men in other generations as it has now been revealed by the Spirit to God's holy apostles and prophets' (Ephesians 3:4-5). In his letter to the Romans he wrote in similar vein: '… according to the revelation of the mystery hidden for long ages past, but now revealed and made known through the prophetic writings by the command of the eternal God …' (Romans 16:25-26). This secret, which God had withheld for so long, but which from that time he chose to disclose to his redeemed people through the prophetic word, is his eternal purpose for the Messiah and for those who belong to him. Paul stated this simply in his Colossian letter when he wrote, 'to them God has chosen to make known … the glorious riches of this mystery, which is Christ in you, the hope of glory' (Colossians 1:27). These words of fathomless meaning, 'Christ in you, the hope of glory', express the heart of God's eternal purpose. It is instructive to note that in the Greek, the 'you' is in the plural. As I have already stated, the divine purpose is to have a saved people in union with the Lord Jesus which may only be described as the organic oneness between head and body.

In most of the terms used to define the relationship between the redeemer and the redeemed, the truth of this spiritual unity is clearly discernible. Let us consider the term most commonly used in the New Testament, that of head and body (*see* Colossians 1:18; Ephesians 4:15-16; 1 Corinthians 12:12-27). It presents a picture of oneness and function. The use of this analogy has no meaning if it is possible to divide head from body, for by their nature, they are unable to live *separate lives*! It is in fact possible to sever head from body but that always results in the cessation of life! If there is to be life, growth and function, head and body belong to each other; they share a common life, a common name, and a common purpose.

Husband and wife, or bridegroom and bride, are also terms employed throughout the Bible to define this relationship (*see* Ephesians 5:22-32; Revelation 19:7; 21:2,9). They present another picture of oneness and love. 'The two shall become one flesh'; two people sharing one life and name, and building one home and family, (*see* Genesis 2:24; Ephesians 5:31). According to the Bible men and women are equal in value and quality but different in function; they complement each other, being two halves of one whole (*see* Genesis 1:27; 2:18-25; Galatians 3:28; 1 Peter 3:7). It is this oneness typified in marriage that is used to define the union between Christ and his people. The marriage service of the prayer book simply states that it was 'instituted in the time of man's innocency to signify the mystical union betwixt Christ and the church'. The Bible begins with an earthly marriage for time between Adam and Eve, and concludes with a heavenly marriage for eternity between the Lamb and the wife of the Lamb; and at its heart is the love story contained in the eight chapters of the Song of Songs.

The vine and the branches is another term which is used to define the relationship between the Lord Jesus and those whom he has saved (*see* John 15:1-16. Compare for example Psalm 80:8-11; Isaiah 5:1-7; 27:1-6; Hosea 10:1). It presents the picture of oneness and fruit. The vine was a well-known symbol of God's covenant people, and the disciples of Jesus would have been acquainted with it from childhood. The claim of Jesus to be that vine is a most remarkable statement and it would have astounded them.

He declared, 'I am the true vine and my Father is the gardener' (John 15:1). His words are popularly understood to mean that he is the trunk or the root, and his people are the branches. But he claims to be, in fact, the whole vine from root to tendrils and fruit, and describes the redeemed as branches within it. When this truth is recognized, the meaning of the oft-repeated injunction 'abide in me, and I in you' becomes more clear.

The temple of God, or the house of God, are further terms employed to describe this oneness (*see* Ephesians 2:20-22; 1 Peter 2:3-5). They present a picture of oneness and service. The Messiah is described as 'the chief corner-stone' or 'a living stone', and those who have been saved through his finished work on the cross are described as 'living stones'. All have been quarried from the same rock. God's temple or house was intended to be a centre for unceasing worship and service: and we as 'living stones are being built into a spiritual house to be a holy priesthood, offering spiritual sacrifices acceptable to God through Jesus Christ'. A house, however, is not constituted by a large number of stones, whether tidily stacked or in a disordered heap; the stones have to be built together according to a design. Furthermore, when the house is built it has to be turned into a home. This must not be overlooked, for a house is not necessarily a home.

It would be impossible to proceed further without drawing attention to another term used to describe the relationship between the Lord and his people. It is the term, the city of God (*see* Revelation 21:1-3, 10-27; Hebrews 12:22; compare Psalm 132:13-14; Psalm 87; Psalm 48). It is found throughout a large part of the Bible and expresses the desire of God's heart for a 'dwelling place'. The fact that God's word concludes with a vision of the city of God is no coincidence, for it reveals the importance of the term. In my view, it is evidence that it should be regarded as a summing up of the other terms. In that version of the city of God, all the materials out of which it has been built have been fused into one eternal work of incredible beauty; the gold, the precious stone, and the pearl, represent the life and the nature of the Lord Jesus as found in those whom he has redeemed. They have been fashioned into an eternal vessel for the glory of God, the fulfilment of the apostle Paul's words 'Christ in you, the hope of glory'.

The new Jerusalem is a remarkable and strange combination of two different ideas, a bride and a city; a bride symbolizing the most intimate relationship known to mankind, a deep union of love, mutual trust and fellowship; a capital city symbolizing government, the headquarters of a national administration and economy. It presents a picture of the bride of the Lamb who has been long-betrothed to the Lamb, finally married to him and taking her place with him on his throne, to reign with him for ever. What work or purposes of love will engage them in the ages to come are not revealed, although it is certain that the creative energy of God will not have faded or deteriorated. If this universe in its fallen state presents such beauty, how much more beautiful will it be when the old order of things has passed away and he makes everything new? What is revealed is their oneness; together they move into the ages to come, joined in an eternal covenant of love. For those who know the Lord, that is enough! It is not necessary to know whether we shall recognize each other, or what we shall wear, or whether we shall eat and drink, or what we shall do? All these questions and many more like them, will be answered in good time. It is enough for the followers of the Lamb to know that they are his, and that he has provided the grace and the power to overcome and reign with him for ever.

This unity into which every true child of God is born of the Spirit, is described by the Lord Jesus as being the same unity that exists between the Father and the Son. In his high priestly prayer, he prayed, 'that all of them may be one, Father, just as you are in me and I am in you. May they also be in us so that the world may believe that you have sent me' (John 17:21). Those who are born of God into this living and organic unity are named in the New Testament as 'the church' or 'the called-out ones'. They have been called by God into an eternal and glorious union with Christ; and called out of a world fragmented and often bitterly divided by racism, colour, nationalism, class consciousness, religious bigotry and prejudice, or even by denominationalism. This union of the redeemed with their Messiah is described in the New Testament as the 'new man', in which 'there is no Greek or Jew, circumcised or uncircumcised, barbarian, Scythian, slave or free, but Christ is all, and is in all' (Colossians 3:11). When the church is divided for any of these reasons, it contradicts the heart of its calling and paralyses its function and growth.

If there had been no fall of man, and sin had not entered into the world, there would have been no church; the church would have been the whole human race. There would have been neither an 'old man' nor a 'new man' but only one kind of man; and that man would have been brought into union with Christ, and would have obtained the glory of God. To use the human terms which God employs, he would have been the bride of Christ, or would have become the home of God by the Spirit, or would have been made the city of God, through which his glory would have shone and through which his government would have been known. This was his eternal purpose. Man, however, sinned and fell short of the glory of God, and God unveiled his matchless and incomparable grace in the story of salvation; and the One who was destined to be bridegroom, husband, and king, also became saviour. This was God's redeeming purpose, and through its accomplishment on Calvary, he saves all those who put their trust in him and restores them to his original purpose.

Sometimes the preaching and the understanding of the good news concerning Jesus the Messiah has been limited to a knowledge of his saving grace; or to an enjoyment of peace and joy through the forgiveness of sins or to an experience of the risen life of the indwelling Christ; or to an appropriation of the anointing and gifts of the Holy Spirit. All these truths are important constituents but they are still less than the whole counsel of God. It is tragic when God's people settle for less than the divine goal for them, and, having experienced his salvation, refuse to press on to win the prize for which he has called them heavenward in Christ Jesus. It is not a matter to be ignored or belittled that believers have been called to be the bride and wife of the Lamb, to become the eternal home and resting place of God, and to be made the holy city, the new Jerusalem, where the throne of his government is eternally located.

The apostle Paul, who had a special understanding of the purpose and calling of God, stated his own position in terms which no one is able to misunderstand, when he wrote,

> 'Not that I have already obtained all this, or have already been made perfect, but I press on to take hold of that for which Christ Jesus took hold of me. Brothers, I do not consider myself yet to have taken hold of it. But one thing I do; Forgetting what is behind and straining towards what is ahead, I press on towards the goal to win the prize for which God has called me heavenwards in Christ Jesus' (Philippians 3:12-14).

Many Christians may be ignorant of the eternal purpose of God and their divine calling but the spiritual forces of darkness are certainly not ignorant of it. The most cunning devices and ferocious powers which they possess are held in reserve for a battle at any time in which they perceive opportunities to frustrate or hinder it. So blind is the hatred of these satanic forces that they even seek to destroy the knowledge of that purpose, working everywhere to keep the people of God in ignorance of it. It is an unceasing and age-long conflict inspired by pride.

At a certain point in a prophecy of Isaiah concerning the king of Babylon, Isaiah saw beyond him to the fallen spirit who energized him, and declared,

> 'How you have fallen from heaven, O morning star, son of the dawn! You have been cast down to the earth, you who once laid low the nations! You said in your heart, "I will ascend to heaven; I will raise my throne above the stars of God; I will sit enthroned on the mount of the assembly, on the utmost heights of the sacred mountain. I will ascend above the tops of the clouds; I will make myself like the Most High" ' (Isaiah 14:12-14).

This prophecy explains the undying hatred and antagonism of Satan for the Messiah and his unceasing opposition of God's purpose for those who have been saved through his death on the cross. The devil has said that he will make himself like the Most High; he intends that he, and not the Messiah, will be enthroned as lord of all.

It is this fact which explains the whole conflict of the ages. Human history is part of that battle between light and darkness, between good and evil, between the truth and the lie, between God and Satan. This battle, in which true and faithful believers find themselves engaged, is not concerned with them as people, for none of them could withstand the enemy for long, if it were not for the grace of God. They have become involved in it because they have been rescued by God from the dominion of darkness, and brought into the kingdom of the Son he loves (*see* Colossians 1:13). For this reason they are a continuous reminder to those forces of darkness that there is a power superior to theirs. Named with the name of Jesus, and bearing his standard, they arouse the insatiable hatred and fury of the adversary's pride. It is a cause for amazement that Satan and his forces have not accepted defeat at God's hand, since the Lord has always turned the devil's devices to good. It is only possible to explain it by 'pride', for there is nothing so blind or so bigoted as pride.

Ezekiel had a similar experience to that of Isaiah when he prophesied concerning the king of Tyre, saying,

'You were the model of perfection, full of wisdom and perfect in beauty. You were in Eden, the garden of God; every precious stone adorned you: ruby, topaz and emerald, chrysolite, onyx and jasper, sapphire, turquoise and beryl. Your settings and mountings were made of gold; on the day you were created they were prepared. You were anointed as a guardian cherub, for so I ordained you. You were on the holy mount of God; you walked among the fiery stones. You were blameless in your ways from the day you were created till wickedness was found in you. Through your widespread trade you were filled with violence, and you sinned. So I drove you in disgrace from the mount of God, and I expelled you, O guardian cherub, from among the fiery stones. Your heart became proud on account of your beauty, and you corrupted your wisdom because of your splendour. So I threw you to the earth ...' (Ezekiel 28:12-17).

It is only possible to understand this prophecy if we look beyond the king of Tyre to the devil who had possessed him and was using him.

These two prophecies are not a complete explanation concerning the origin of sin and evil but provide us with a sufficient explanation until that day when all secrets will be revealed. It should be a source of unending strength and encouragement to those who are disciples of the Lord Jesus to realize that if the destructive and hateful design of Satan is focused upon God's eternal purpose, the redeeming purpose of God is also centred on it. The Lord will not fail those whom he has redeemed, nor will he forsake them, for he has provided in their salvation sufficient power and grace to bring them to his goal. This was the truth John stated when he wrote, 'for everyone born of God has overcome the world. This is the victory that has overcome the world, even our faith. Who is it that overcomes the world? Only he who believes that Jesus is the Son of God' (1 John 5:4-5).

Christians often become excited about details of prophecy and yet remain ignorant of God's eternal purpose which is revealed in that prophetic word. They are unaware that it explains human history in the light of the divine goal and has an intensely practical relevance for every aspect of their lives; few subjects could have more importance or more significance for them. It is possible to treat the word of prophecy as a mere catalogue of dates, times, and predicted battles and, becoming absorbed with prophetic details, miss the supremely important message it conveys.

6. *I am the Alpha and the Omega*

At the beginning of the Bible a short phrase occurs ten times in the first twenty-five verses, which represents an important biblical principle; it is the phrase 'after their kind' (*see* Genesis 1:11, 12, 21, 24, 25). From it we learn that the reproduction and the fulfilment of every created thing is determined by 'its kind'; or, to state it in another way, their origin determines their destiny.

Throughout the Bible, the word of prophecy reveals this principle and applies it to both natural and spiritual life. All the prophets declare that whatever has its origin in fallen man will fall short of the glory of God; and whatever has its origin in God and is born of him will reach his glory. It was a God-given prophetic insight which enabled them to spell out in simple language the basic and unchanging law that sin unerringly leads to corruption and death, to ultimate failure and loss; and the saving grace and power of God unfailingly lead to eternal life, to ultimate success and glory. On whatever level this principle operates, the determining factor is always 'origin'; it is the same whether it is on the personal, national, or international level. This is one of those areas in which it is easy to be deceived, for the work of fallen man may be noble, beautiful, cultured or may even be the work of genius. Nevertheless it will not be found in eternity, because it belongs to that old order of things which will pass away in the day when the Lord makes everything new. Only that which has its origin in God will endure through time and through eternity; all else will fail or decay and pass away.

It is not essential to have reached a high state of spiritual maturity to recognize that this truth of the prophetic word has an intensely practical significance for all who belong to God. Few truths could hold more relevance for them than the prophetic warning concerning 'origins'. In fact, there is no area of life on which it has not some light to shed, or some vital understanding to impart. A major part of the battle that surrounds the followers of the Lamb has been won, if the origin of their 'Christian life', their 'Christian service' and their 'church life' is right. Those who are born of God will not only have the grace and power of God made available to them, but will also have within them the life of the Spirit – the essence of victory. Within their spiritual birth and life are the genes of glory!

It is for this reason that the apostle Peter writes, 'Therefore, my brothers, be all the more eager to make *your calling and election sure.* For if you do these things you will never fall, and you will receive a rich welcome into the eternal kingdom of our Lord and Saviour Jesus Christ' (2 Peter 1:10-11, italics mine). Once this principle is clearly understood the many subtle devices of God's adversary, which would otherwise deceive, delude or sidetrack, will be discerned in time, and the real spirit which inspires modern ideologies, politics, education and morality will be exposed. This will be even more important for those who will live during the last stages of world history. During that time many new and 'enlightened' theories concerning the basic constituents of life such as sexual purity, the marriage relationship, the family unit, the sexuality of men and women, abortion, euthanasia, etc., will make their appearance with devastating impact upon the educational systems and life of the nations.

This principle which is found throughout the Scriptures
is most clearly expressed in the New Testament in the
words of the apostle Paul when he wrote,

> 'For as in Adam all die, so in Christ all will be made alive ...
> So it is written: "The first man Adam became a living being";
> the last Adam, a life-giving spirit ... The first man was of the
> dust of the earth, the second man from heaven. As was the
> earthly man, so are those who are of the earth; and as is the
> man from heaven, so also are those who are of heaven ... I
> declare to you, brothers, that flesh and blood cannot inherit
> the kingdom of God, nor does the perishable inherit the
> imperishable. Listen, I tell you a mystery: we will not all
> sleep, but we will all be changed ... For the trumpet will
> sound, the dead will be raised imperishable, and we will be
> changed' (1 Corinthians 15:22, 45, 47-48, 50-52).

Those whose life originates in the first Adam are living
beings but are of the earth. They belong to that realm of
fallen and perishable flesh and blood which, by its nature,
is unable to inherit the kingdom of God. Those whose life
originates in the last Adam have been born of the Spirit,
and have received eternal life. They are of heaven and in
the final stage of their redemption even their bodies will
be changed and become imperishable and immortal. In
both cases, their origins determine their characters and
destinies.

The Lord Jesus used simple words to state this truth
when he spoke to Nicodemus, and said, 'That which is
born of the flesh is flesh; and that which is born of the
Spirit is spirit. Marvel not that I said unto thee, Ye must
be born again' (John 3:6-7 AV). Those who are born of the
flesh remain in the realm of the flesh. They may be
cultured, educated, religious, or even highly christianized
but if they were only born of the flesh, they will have to
remain flesh. It is impossible for them to evolve into the
realm of the Spirit, for they have to be born of the Spirit to
enter that realm. Only those who are born of the Spirit are

able to live and walk by the Spirit and produce the fruit of the Spirit (*see* Galatians 5:16-26). If they were born only of the flesh, that kind of origin will characterize their life and development and determine their destiny. On the other hand, if they have been born of the Spirit, through the saving work of the Lord Jesus (*see* John 3:14-17), that spiritual origin will also characterize their life and development and determine their glorious destiny.

This is why Paul warns Christians in his Galatian letter, 'Do not be deceived, God is not mocked; for whatever a man sows, this he will also reap. For the one who sows to his own flesh shall from the flesh reap corruption, but the one who sows to the Spirit shall from the Spirit reap eternal life' (Galatians 6:7-8 NASB). A person may be born of the Spirit but may be sowing to his flesh, with sad consequences, and it is this which is the burden of Paul's warning. It is not unduly critical to observe that much Christian life and service is to be found in this category.

It is even more starkly and boldly expressed in the words, 'everything that does not come from faith is sin' (Romans 14:23). Since faith is 'not from ourselves' but 'is the gift of God' (*see* Ephesians 2:8), this sentence is a re-stating of the truth that everything is trapped within the hopeless realm of sin and death unless it has its origin in God. There is no exit from that realm except through a living and God-given faith. That is the only means by which a person is able to be made one with God, to know his will, enjoy his life and power, and experience his working. Everything done apart from faith remains in the domain of sin, and is unable to inherit God's eternal kingdom and glory.

There are two trees which characterize the whole history of man and interpret the Bible. The first is the tree of life, which appears in the early chapters of Genesis and reappears in the final chapters of the Revelation of John (*see* Genesis 2:9; 3:22-24; Revelation 22:2, 14; compare

Ezekiel 47:7,12). The second is the tree of the knowledge of good and evil which is found only in the first chapters of Genesis but whose effects are found throughout the Bible (*see* Genesis 2:9,17; 3:1-19).

It is my belief that there was an actual garden of Eden with two actual trees located at or near its centre. It is also as certain, in my view, that those trees represented spiritual realities to Adam and Eve, and have continued to represent those realities throughout the ages of time. It was not the eating of certain fruit which had such disastrous and enduring consequences for humanity, but what it revealed – a wilful decision directed against God. On the most obvious level, it expressed distrust and disobedience, but on the deepest level, a deliberate and knowing act of rebellion.

In the Bible, trees are often used to symbolize the life and character of men (*see* Psalm 1:3; 37:35; 52:8; 92:12-14; Isaiah 61:3; Jeremiah 17:5-8; Hosea 14:5-7). The tree of life represents eternal life, the life of God which he makes available to man in the person of the Son; it is a life derived from God and lived through God. It also symbolizes a human nature and constitution which is God-centred, God-conscious and God-dependent. In this sense, it symbolizes Christ, the last Adam, the man from heaven, and those who have been made alive in him.

The tree of the knowledge of good and evil represents a very different kind of life and constitution; it represents Adam, the first man, and those who die in him. Satan uttered a half-truth when he spoke to Eve and said, ' "You will not surely die" … "For God knows that when you eat of it your eyes will be opened, and you will be like God, knowing good and evil" ' (Genesis 3:4-5). It was true that the taking of the fruit of the tree of the knowledge of good and evil did not result in immediate physical death, although that was the point at which it made its debut with mankind. It was, however, untrue that there would be no immediate death. The death which transpired on that day was a spiritual death, far more terrible in its consequences than physical death; it was the death of the kind of person God intended man to be. Instead of becoming the bride of Christ, or the dwelling place of God in the spirit, man became a self-centred, self-conscious, and self-sufficient creature; a constitution and a condition which precludes true and lasting happiness and joy. Satan had said, 'You will become like God knowing good and evil', and man became a 'demi-god' with everything centred in himself, and in his own genius, knowledge and resources.

The bloodied, tearstained pages of man's long history provide the evidence for the failure of that kind of man. No amount of human brilliance, power, or will, has been able to overcome the basic problems of mankind and produce 'the golden age'. After at least 6,000 years of human endeavour and aspiration, modern man is as far away as ever from such a goal. His origin has determined both his character and his destiny. The word of prophecy reveals how that kind of man and constitution originated and developed. It also reveals another kind of man represented by the tree of life; a man saved and remade by the grace of God, who, having been born of God, is being transformed into his likeness. His origin is also determining his character and destiny.

These two trees represent, therefore, two different kinds of men, Adam and Christ, and those who either die in Adam, or have been made alive in Christ; and both trees are reproducing 'after their own kind'! In the final vision of the Bible, we see only the tree of life, full of life-giving fruit and healing properties. The tree of the knowledge of good and evil appears to have shrivelled up and died, for it is nowhere mentioned in those chapters. It has passed away with the old order of things, along with death and mourning, crying and pain.

There are also two cities which characterize the history

of man and interpret the Bible; the first city is Jerusalem, and the second is Babylon. It would be impossible to list all the references to them in the Bible for reasons of space but the name Jerusalem occurs 812 times, apart from the numerous other names by which she is known, such as 'Zion' or 'the holy city'. Babylon and Babel occur 285 times. The first appear in the early chapters of the Bible and from that point onwards there are only two cities in the sight of God into which all men are divided; there is no third city. In the final analysis everything is explained by the different origin and nature of these cities.

Babylon, which in Hebrew is always known as Babel, represents the genius and prowess of man; she is the product of man from beginning to end, and the sum of his glory. At the zenith of her history she became one of the greatest cities in the annals of mankind and justly famed. Her hanging gardens, her fine avenues and boulevards, her commercial centres and banking houses, her famous iron gates, her palaces and temples, and her man-made canals permitting sea-faring ships to sail from the Persian Gulf into the centre of the city, made her appear to be timeless and indestructible. To all of this must be added the fact that she was the capital of the most powerful and extensive empire of the day. For these reasons God chose her to symbolize the resourcefulness, ingenuity and hopelessness of fallen man.

Babel was man's first attempt to form a 'united nations organization' and to regain a lost paradise by uniting earth to heaven. She began as a determination in the heart of her builders expressed in their words, 'Come, let us build ourselves a city, with a tower that reaches to the heavens, so that we may make a name for ourselves and not be scattered over the face of the whole earth' (Genesis 11:4). The name Babel, which in Hebrew means 'confusion', was probably a pun based on an original Assyrian name, *Bab Illi*, which means 'the gate of God'. The builders of

Babel considered their work to be the solution to the basic problems that mankind was facing. They determined that it should overcome the consequences of his fall, and be the divine gateway into a human paradise and the Golden Age. They called their city 'the Gate of God', but God called it 'confusion'. It is not difficult to understand the reason why Babylon was chosen to be the symbol of fallen man. She expresses all human endeavour to produce a 'Golden Age', a Utopia, through man's own resources and energies without a revolutionary and radical change in his nature and constitution. In this sense, Babylon is the sum total of human history, endeavour, and failure. To the undiscerning eye, she is magnificent. Filled with all the finest works of man, she is a monument to his fallen genius. Yet Babylon is doomed to failure because she is without foundations; her origin has determined her destiny.

Jerusalem represents the saving grace and power of God; she is the work of God from beginning to end. She began with his choice, is preserved by his love and faithfulness, and ends with his glory. Jerusalem was chosen without any of the natural advantages which are normally associated with a capital city. She had no harbour, no navigable river, no canals which would permit ships to sail into her centre; she was not situated on any great commercial crossroads; she had no hanging gardens or fine processional avenues; she had the most precarious water supply of any capital city. Compared with Babylon, Jerusalem was an insignificant provincial town in the Judean mountains. It is clear that she was chosen to convey a reality, 'not of this world'; to represent eternal and divine truth and convey the light of God to this world.

In a real sense, the story of Jerusalem began with the story of Abraham. It is revealed in the letter to the Hebrews that, 'By faith Abraham, when he was called, obeyed to go out unto a place which he was to receive for an inheritance; ... for he looked for the city which hath the foundations, whose builder and maker is God' (Hebrews 11:8-10 RV). Stephen, describing the same event, said that, 'The God of Glory appeared to our father Abraham while he was still in Mesopotamia ... "Leave your country and your people," God said, "and go to the land I will show you" ' (Acts 7:2-3). In what manner Abraham was given an understanding of God's eternal purpose is not explained in the Bible, but in seeing the God of Glory, *he saw the city which hath the foundations* which alone would express the glory of God throughout eternity.

Abraham was never the same again; he was spoiled for any human and earthly city. He had been born in the Babylonian complex of cities, in Ur of the Chaldees. When, however, he saw the Lord it became clear to him that Ur was without foundations in spite of its education and refinement, its advanced and sophisticated standards, and its apparent indestructibility. Turning his back on it, he left it never to return. By God's grace, Abraham became, through his faith and obedience to God, a citizen of that other city which has *the* foundations whose architect and builder is divine.

In principle all true believers have the same history as Abraham: they are saved by the eyes of their hearts being opened to behold their God and Saviour, and their citizenship is transferred from Babylon to Jerusalem by a new and spiritual birth. God has changed their origin and therefore their destiny. Psalm 87 expresses this truth clearly:

'He has set his foundation on the holy mountain; the Lord loves the gates of Zion more than all the dwellings of Jacob. Glorious things are said of you, O city of God: 'I will record Rahab and Babylon among those who acknowledge me – Philistia too, and Tyre, along with Cush – and will say, "This one was born in Zion". Indeed, of Zion it will be said, "This one and that one were born in her, and the Most High himself will establish her." The Lord will write in the register of the peoples: "This one was born in Zion." As they make music they will sing, "All my fountains are in you." '

Although originally born in Egypt, Babylon, Philistia or elsewhere, those who have been redeemed by God and belong to him are registered as being born in Zion. Their former origin is cancelled and expunged from the record. They have become members of God's Zion, and have to learn the secret of their new birth that 'all my fountains are in thee'. They are able to sing with John Newton, the redeemed slave driver:

> 'Saviour, if of Zion's city,
> I through grace a member am,
> Let the world deride or pity,
> I will glory in Thy name.
> Failing is the worldling's pleasure,
> All his boasted pomp and show,
> Solid joys and lasting treasure,
> None but Zion's children know'.

The story of these two cities begins in Genesis chapters 11 and 12 and continues through the divine record until it reaches its climax in the final chapters of the book of Revelation. Those chapters reveal the ultimate issues in bold colours: Babylon with all its wealth, power, pomp and show is destroyed, never to reappear (Revelation 17-19); and Jerusalem comes down out of heaven having the glory of God, to reign for ever with the Messiah (Revelation 21-22). Their different origins have determined their different characters and their different destinies.

A further illustration of this principle is found in the two sons of Abraham, Ishmael and Isaac. God gave Abraham no ordinary promise when he predicted that he would have a son; that his seed would become as multitudinous as the dust of the earth, as the stars of the sky, and as the sand on the seashore; and that in his seed all the families of the earth would be blessed (*see* Genesis 13:16; 15:4-5; 17:15-17; 22:16-18).

The problem for Abraham and Sarah was the way in which such a promise could be naturally fulfilled. Their problem consisted of two main factors, Sarah's infertility, and her age. She was then in her early seventies. For some years they both waited in faith for God to perform the impossible and fulfil the first stage of the promise – the birth of a son, but nothing happened.

Sarah would have been about seventy-five years of age when she reconsidered the situation in the light of the divine promise and of her physical condition. She made a proposal that Abraham should take Hagar, her Egyptian bondslave, and have the promised child through her – a proposal which was entirely permissible according to the law of the day. It was a plan produced by the impeccable logic of common sense; it joined together the word and the purpose of God, the ideas of contemporary society, and the actual circumstances and conditions of the people to whom the promise of God had been given. Although Sarah's scheme offered an apparently perfect solution to their difficulty, it was not of God, and was in fact to have disastrous and time-lasting consequences. It was 'the mind of the flesh' in action and not the operation of a living faith. It resulted in the birth of Ishmael. He was born in the ordinary way, according to a human plan, and represents the mind of the flesh, with its natural strength, its willpower and its energy.

Thirteen years later when Sarah was eighty-nine years of age and Abraham was ninety-nine, although impossible by human standards, Sarah conceived and Isaac was born. He was born as the result of a divinely given promise, through the power of the Holy Spirit, and represents the mind of the Spirit. These two sons of

Abraham symbolize different principles of origin, nature and living. Their destiny also differs, for one is unable to inherit and is 'cast out', and the other inherits and participates in the fulfilment of God's eternal purpose (*see* Genesis 16:1-16; 17:17-21; 21:1-20; compare Galatians 4:21-31; 5:16-25; Romans 8:1-17).

Ishmael may have had more of Abraham's looks and personality in him than Isaac, but a divine veto rested upon him because he originated with the flesh, and he was unable to share in the inheritance which God had promised to his father. On the other hand, Isaac may have had few or none of Abraham's looks and characteristic traits, yet he inherited and became part of God's city because he was born through God's word and his effectual power. Again, origin determined destiny.

It is possible to apply this truth to every aspect of not only Christian life and service but also to the life and work of the church. For instance, the origin of our salvation is to be found wholly in God. There is not a vestige of it which originates in fallen man. It was in the mind of God that the plan of salvation was conceived; it was the undying love of God which carried it into effect; it was the Son of God who accomplished it by his work on the cross; and it is the Holy Spirit who draws uncaring sinners to God, melting the hardness of their hearts, granting them repentance, imparting to them the gift of faith, and causing them to be born of God.

The apostle Paul stated this truth when he wrote,

'But because of his great love for us, God, who is rich in mercy, made us alive with Christ even when we were dead in transgressions ... For it is by grace you have been saved, through faith – and this not from yourselves, it is the gift of God – not by works, so that no-one can boast. For we are God's workmanship, created in Christ Jesus ...' (Ephesians 2:4-5; 8-10).

A salvation which has its origin in man, in his good works, his natural character, his willpower, or his religious observance, is not the salvation of God but humanistic religion. It is an 'Ishmael' and not an 'Isaac', and is predestined to fall short of the glory of God.

Likewise the origin of the Christian life is in Christ; in fact, Christ *is* the Christian life. The term 'Christian life' appears nowhere in the Bible; the only *Christian* life known to the Bible, and to the New Testament in particular, is *eternal* life. God has given us eternal life in his Son and when we believe on him, we receive his eternal life. This is the Christian life, which we receive in the person of Christ. For example, the Lord Jesus declared, 'I am the way and the truth and *the life*. No-one comes to the Father except through me' (John 14:6, italics mine); and John wrote, 'And this is the testimony: God has given us eternal life, and *this life is in his Son. He who has the Son has life*; he who does not have the Son of God does not have life' (1 John 5:11, 12, italics mine); Paul in his letter to the Philippians wrote, 'For to me, to *live is Christ*' (Philippians 1:21, italics mine), and in his letter to the Colossians stated this truth again in the words, 'For you died, and your life is now hidden with Christ in God. When *Christ, who is your life* ...' (Colossians 3:3,4, italics mine).

This is where some Christians make their basic mistake. Although they recognize the truth that they were unable to save themselves and needed to receive Christ as their salvation, they fail to recognize the equally important truth that they are unable to live the Christian life of themselves; they need to experience Christ as their life. They try to live the Christian life in their own strength with natural resources, seeking to emulate the pattern as seen in him and his apostles. Their motives are often noble and good but that kind of Christian life is natural in its origin; it is an 'Ishmael' and not an 'Isaac'. It is a natural life dressed up to appear as the Christian life. Since the principle of the natural life is corruption and death, it becomes an exhaustion and even a revulsion to the honest child of God.

This kind of 'christianized' natural life is artificially concocted. It is like tying apples on to the branches of an apple tree in order to make it appear fruitful and useful; its true condition is useless and barren, for the apples soon shrivel since their life is not drawn from the tree. The fruit of the Spirit is in a different dimension. It is not produced by attaching to one's natural life the Christian qualities of love, joy, peace, patience, goodness, faithfulness, gentleness, and self-control. It is produced by recognizing and obeying the law of the Spirit of life in Christ Jesus since that fruit will always be the spontaneous outcome of his indwelling (*see* Galatians 5:22-25, Romans 8:2).

This is the meaning of the words of the Lord Jesus when he said, 'Abide in Me, and I in you. As the branch cannot bear fruit of itself, unless it abides in the vine, so neither can you, unless you abide in Me. I am the vine, you are the branches; he who abides in Me, and I in him, he bears much fruit; for apart from Me you can do nothing' (John 15:4,5 NASB).

God has crucified with Christ the natural life and all its qualities, both good and bad; that is his estimate of it, (*see* Galatians 2:20; Romans 6:8-14; compare Mark 8:34-35; Galatians 5:24). True believers should leave that life where the Lord has placed it, on Christ's cross and in his grave. If God has terminated it by the death of the Lord Jesus, there is no value in his children seeking to resurrect and 'christianize' it. They have a new life in Christ with new potentialities and abilities and a new destiny. God has made them alive together with Christ that they might learn to walk in the newness of his life, and experience that in Christ, he has provided everything necessary to reach his goal.

Even the physical bodies of the redeemed will be ultimately changed by this union with Christ. If their origin is in Christ and found no longer in Adam, their redemption will be completed when they receive the same kind of body as he has; imperishable, glorious, powerful and spiritual (*see* 1 Corinthians 15:42-44). The Lord Jesus referred to the redemption of the body when he spoke to his disciples concerning the possibility of martyrdom and said, 'but not a hair of your head will perish' (Luke 21:18). The apostle Paul explained it in the words '... but we will all be changed – in a flash, in the twinkling of an eye, at the last trumpet. For the trumpet will sound, the dead will be raised imperishable, and we will be changed ...' (1 Corinthians 15:51-52). So tremendous is this miracle that even when the body of a true believer has returned to the dust for thousands of years, it will be brought back in glory, not in its original perishable state, but redeemed to God's original purpose for mankind.

All true Christian service and work has its origin in God. When it begins with him, it is sustained by him and will end in his glory. The Lord Jesus revealed the unchanging law of spiritual success in the service and the work of God when he said,

> 'Truly, truly, I say to you, unless a grain of wheat falls into the earth and dies, it remains by itself alone; but if it dies, it bears much fruit. He who loves his life loses it; and he who hates his life in this world shall keep it to life eternal. If anyone serve Me, let him follow Me; and where I am, there shall My servant also be; if anyone serves Me, the Father will honor him' (John 12:24-26 NASB).

If we would know that kind of success in our life of service, we have to follow him through death into resurrection, for there is no alternative way. Much Christian work has originated not with God but with human ability, natural strength and with worldly ideas. It is work performed *for* God in the name of Christ, which uses his word, but is not *his* work. It is a sad fact that the way, the methods, and the psychology of this world often lurk behind a facade of Christian service; it is the mind of the flesh masquerading as the servant of the Lord. It is impossible for that kind of work to please the Lord, for it is an 'Ishmael' and not an 'Isaac'.

The same factors are apparent in church life, for so much of that which is called 'the church' is not the true church but the world dressed up as the church! The church was born at Pentecost and came in the life of her risen and glorified head poured out through the person of the Holy Spirit. That was her origin and, as long as she obeyed the law of her life, she turned the world upside down. The life of the Messiah produced a living, 'organic' community which was spiritually sensitive, loving, powerful and dynamic; a body through which he could speak and work. In the history of the church this character has always been evident in every new move of the Holy Spirit, until the flesh has grieved the Spirit, quenching him and turning his living work into a dead monument to past glories. The Holy Spirit came to produce the body of Christ, and not to create a formal, impersonal and institutional organization; that was formed by the world and the mind of the flesh and is an 'Ishmael' which all through history has despised and persecuted the 'Isaac' of God.

As I have already stated, the question will arise in some minds as to how these last two chapters relate to prophecy and the answer is that they represent essential aspects of prophetic ministry. There is little value in an exhaustive knowledge of prophetic details concerning coming events if there is no understanding of God's eternal purpose and of God's warning concerning origins.

In the last chapter of the last book of the Bible, the Lord Jesus said, 'I am the Alpha and the Omega, the First and the Last, the Beginning and the End' (Revelation 22:13;

see also Revelation 21:6; 1:8,17). In giving this final word of prophecy, the ascended, glorified Messiah emphasizes the importance of this truth concerning 'origins'. If he is the Alpha, the first letter of the Greek alphabet, he is also the Omega, its last letter, and also all the intervening letters. It is impossible for him to be the Omega if he is not the Alpha; he will be the Last, only if he has been the First; and he will finish in glory only that which he began in grace. This word has a solemn and a practical relevance for all who are born of God, for there is no area of personal, national or international life, on which it has not some light to shed, and especially on the modern trends in politics, education, morality and religion.

If the origin of our salvation, our Christian life, our Christian service and work, or our church life, is God in Christ, then it will follow that all his grace and power is made available to us. He will guard us, change us, empower us, deliver us, and guide us to his desired goal. It will make no difference to those who follow the Lamb the whole way that all the forces of evil and darkness conspire together against them, or that fierce trials, or much tribulation, or even martyrdom await them. If the path began with the Messiah, it will end in his triumph and on his throne; it will end with unimaginable joy in the glory of God.

7. The times of the Gentiles

The Bible is unique in the world of literature. No other book has presented an outline of world history, predicted thousands of years before its fulfilment, which has proved, until the present time, to be exact in its accuracy. Nor is there any reason to fear that it will fail in what remains to be fulfilled. This is a further aspect of biblical prophecy which we have now to consider. Some of my readers who have equated prophecy only with that type of prediction will feel that they are on more familiar ground in this chapter than they were in the preceding two. Nevertheless, an understanding of the principles referred to in those chapters is fundamental to a balanced view of this aspect of prophecy.

Through his prophetic word, God gives his people an outline of world history *in the light of his eternal purpose*, and not a general history of the world's empires and nations. That fact can never be over-emphasized. Everything concerning the history of the world which is essential to the understanding and fulfilment of his purpose is included, and everything which has no direct bearing on that goal is excluded. Some of the world's greatest empires and civilizations are not even mentioned, such as the Chinese Empire, whilst others, such as the Egyptian or the Persian Empires, are included only because they have touched his elect people in some degree.

Certain passages of these prophecies are so detailed

and accurate in their description of successive world empires, and of some of the main personalities and events which have shaped them, that liberal scholarship considered it impossible for them to have been written *before* the events described and has formed the theory that they must have been written afterwards in the guise of prophecy.

A classic example of such a prophecy is the prediction in Daniel chapter 8 of Alexander the Great, the division of his empire into four separate kingdoms, and the emergence from one of them of the Seleucid king, Antiochus IV Epiphanes, as the original type of the antichrist. A further example is to be found in Daniel chapter 11 which covers the same ground as Daniel 8 but concentrates in detail upon the Ptolemaic Kingdom of the south centred on Egypt, and the Seleucid Kingdom of the north centred on Syria, culminating in the reign of the same Seleucid king, Antiochus IV. In my view, it is an open question whether scholars who make such suggestions would themselves stoop to such an unethical and dishonest level of conduct but it it highly questionable to impute to servants of the Lord from another age fraudulent and dishonest motives and suggest that they practised a hoax on God's people. It remains as unacceptable even when it is excused as resulting from fear of tyrannical authorities.

The outline of world history presented by the prophetic word holds a profound relevance for God's people which they would be wise to consider. It is not the mere prediction of events, nor the chronological sequence of their fulfilment, which holds the relevance for them, but the revelation that truth will ultimately win. Since God is truth and it is impossible for him to be defeated or to be destroyed, truth must triumph. It is written, 'God *is* light, in him there is no darkness at all' (1 John 1:5, italics mine). To have made this statement is infinitely more significant than to have written that 'God gives light' or that 'God enlightens people'. The Lord Jesus declared, 'I am … the truth' (John 14:6). None of his disciples would dispute that he preached the truth and that the truth was revealed in him, but the comprehensive claim – 'I am the truth' – places the whole matter in another dimension. If the Lord Jesus Christ is the truth, it is invincible and its ultimate vindication is certain. It would make no difference even if all the forces of hell were to combine together against it and the whole world were to become demonized.

John wrote in the beginning of his gospel, 'In him was life, and that life was the light of men. The light shines in the darkness, but the darkness has not overcome it' (John 1:4,5; margin). Although there is a 'prince of this world' and 'the world lies in the evil one'; although there are evil principalities, powers and world rulers of this darkness who are terrible in their nature; although there is a 'prince of the power of the air', a spirit who energizes the sons of disobedience: none of them were able to overcome the Lord Jesus as the light of God, and extinguish that light. He triumphed, defeating them all by finishing the work on the cross which God had given him to do, and as absolute victor has sat down at his right hand (*see* John 16:11; 1 John 5:19; Ephesians 2:2; 6:12).

Furthermore, in outlining the course of human history the Spirit of God has no hesitation in drawing back the veil and revealing the evil devices and the bestial cruelty of the forces which dominate the human scene. Many fearful and dark things, which are satanic in their origin, are predicted in its course. They will reach their climax during the last days in demonically inspired ideological, political and economic systems, and will culminate in the person and rule of the antichrist, the man of sin. All of this is not prophesied to make God's people fearful and depressed. On the contrary, it is revealed that they might be encouraged, strengthened and comforted. Nothing could hold more encouragement and comfort for them than the jubilant proclamation of the word of prophecy that 'the Most High rules in the affairs of men', or that 'his throne is for ever and ever', or that the Messiah is enthroned at God's right hand and has all authority in heaven and on earth.

It is a remarkable fact that the Spirit of God never reveals the dark and evil nature of future events without forcefully declaring the absolute sovereignty of God and of the Lamb. He declares that it is the Most High, the king of the universe, who brings men to positions of supreme authority and who also removes them, whether it is good men or evil, god-fearing men or atheists. It is he who ordains the rise to power of empires, nations and even ideologies, and who disposes of them when their appointed time has arrived. It is a cause for real encouragement that whenever the Holy Spirit depicts the more dark and fearsome events of the last days, he always presents a glorious and joyful vision of the purpose of God finally fulfilled: the Lamb and the wife of the Lamb married; the holy city coming down out of heaven having the glory of God; a new heaven and a new earth in which righteousness dwells; and the earth filled with the knowledge of his glory as the waters cover the sea (*see* Revelation 19:7; 21:10-11; 2 Peter 3:13; Habakkuk 2:14).

The achievement of that end is as certain as every other phase which God has outlined and which has come to pass. This fact should be a source of perennial strength to us, for at times the future may appear to be dark and foreboding. The Lord has revealed these events beforehand for our encouragement. When they begin to be fulfilled, his children will be able to understand that the one who has revealed the end from the beginning is in control of all and is working out his purpose through them with a glorious end in view. In this way they will receive the comfort and strength needed to overcome. John wrote,

'You, dear children, are from God and have overcome them, because the one who is in you is greater than the one who is in the world' (1 John 4:4).

If we are 'from God' there is no need to fear either that which is coming on the world, or the spirit who is in the world and energizes it, for the satisfying reason that we are on the winning side! Furthermore, it is impossible to receive the strength to overcome and see the Lord face to face, unless we have a revelation of his indwelling, for 'the One who is *in you* is greater ....' The word of prophecy was not given that we might be comforted but that we might be prepared and made ready.

The Lord has outlined the course of history because it is important that his people should know what stage has been reached in its progress, and be prepared and equipped for what lies ahead. Difficult as it is to imagine, there are Christians who appear to believe that they are automatically prepared and ready for the last days and for the coming of the Lord if they have been saved and have a knowledge of the Bible and Christian doctrine. To be saved is essential, and to possess sound doctrine and a knowledge of the Bible is vital. More than that, however, is required to be prepared for those days; unconfessed sin has to be put away whatever the cost; the basic issues of self-centredness, self-love, and self-preservation have to be settled; a living practical faith in his lordship is necessary in order to experience all that has been provided in him; and an experience of the anointing of the Holy Spirit is essential to be properly equipped to fulfil his will and to do his work.

The truth will win, and all those born of the truth, who have been made 'light in the Lord', will be enabled steadfastly to endure and also win. In the final analysis it will be the measure in which the redeemed of the Lord have lived in the light, have been faithful to the light, and

have known that light dwelling in them, that will determine the measure of their triumph and glory. The Lord
Jesus revealed the nature of this light when he declared, 'I
am the light of the world. Whoever follows me will never
walk in darkness, but will have the light *of life*' (John 8:12,
italics mine). It is important to note that the Lord
promises 'the light of life' and not, as would be expected,
'the light of knowledge'. This light and truth is not
academic in nature but is the light of his life and presence,
and is the difference between 'the tree of the knowledge
of good and evil' and 'the tree of life'. If we live and walk
in the light, we will have nothing to fear. Neither a nuclear
way, nor an antichrist, nor demonic political and economic systems, nor all the satanic beings in the universe, are
able to destroy him, or those who are in him. Even if they
are called on to be martyrs, it will make no difference to
the fact that not a hair of their heads will perish. In one
sense, it is immaterial whether we live or die, for when the
Lord comes we shall all be changed, and will be together
with him for ever; the truth will have won!

Daniel is one of the most outstanding servants of the
Lord whose life and ministry is recorded in the Bible. He
was born of nobility and, according to one tradition, was a
prince of the royal house of David. It was certainly his
aristocratic birth which ensured that as a teenager of great
promise he was included by Nebuchadnezzar in the
deportation from Jerusalem to Babylon in 606 B.C. (*see*
Daniel 1:3-6; compare 2 Kings 24:1-16). He was made a
eunuch and given three years of special education in
Babylon with the aim of placing him in the royal service.

God greatly honoured and favoured Daniel because of
his refusal to compromise on any spiritual issue. He not
only entered that service but also rose from one influential
position to another through the successive reigns of
Babylonian and Persian kings, until he was made supreme
administrator of the whole Persian Empire. He was a man

of supreme faith, of divinely given insight and wisdom, and of costly intercession, who in his long life (he lived into his nineties) never wavered in his total commitment to the Lord. It was to this man, more than to any other, that God chose to reveal 'the times of the Gentiles'. In a series of visions he saw by the Spirit the course of world history in the light of the coming kingdom of God.

It was the Lord Jesus who used the term 'the times of the Gentiles' when he said, 'Jerusalem will be trampled on by the Gentiles until the times of the Gentiles are fulfilled' (Luke 21:24). It is a term which denotes the Gentile domination of the Jewish people, and of history in general, in the outworking of God's sovereign will. It ought not to be confused with the term used by the apostle Paul, 'the fulness of the Gentiles', or 'the full number of the Gentiles', which refers to God's saving purpose for the Gentiles (*see* Romans 11:25). The times of the Gentiles is a period of history which began with the Babylonian Empire and has lasted until our day.

The times of the Gentiles are outlined in a number of visions given to Daniel at different times in his life but covering the same period of history. The first of the dream visions was in fact given to King Nebuchadnezzar when Daniel was in his early twenties, and is fundamental to the understanding of the others. It was a vision of

'an enormous, dazzling statue, awesome in appearance. The head of the statue was made of pure gold, its chest and arms of silver, its belly and thighs of bronze, its legs of iron, its feet partly of iron and partly of baked clay. While you were watching, a rock was cut out, but not by human hands. It struck the statue on its feet of iron and clay and smashed them. Then the iron, the clay, the bronze, the silver, and the gold were broken to pieces at the same time and became like chaff on a threshing floor in the summer. The wind swept them away without leaving a trace. But the rock that struck the statue became a huge mountain and filled the whole earth' (Daniel 2:31-35).

Daniel was given the interpretation of the vision by God. There would be four successive world empires which in God's sight constitute the heart of human history, and which would influence all civilization that would follow to the end of time. During the course of that period the Messiah would appear, and his appearance would both smash the man-made statue into pieces and introduce the eternal kingdom of God (*see* Daniel 2:36-35).

King Nebuchadnezzar of Babylon (606-562 B.C.) was the head of gold. Thus we learn that the times of the Gentiles began with the subjugation of the Jewish people by Babylon. It becomes clear then that the second empire and the successor to Babylon, was Persia; the third empire, the successor to Persia, was Greece; and the fourth empire, the successor to Greece, was Rome – 'strong as iron' and 'crushing and breaking all the others'.

The identification of the fourth empire as Rome, has been questioned by some scholars who have suggested that it is either the Greek Empire, or a revived Babylon in the last days. In my view, the question is settled by the statement that, 'In the time of those kings, the God of heaven will set up a kingdom that will never be destroyed, nor will it be left to another people. It will crush all those kingdoms and bring them to an end, but it will itself endure for ever' (Daniel 2:24). The first coming of the Messiah, that 'rock cut out, but not by human hands', was in the period of the Roman Empire; and his second coming will be at the end of the period of modern civilization which is the outcome of that empire, but which also includes many characteristics of the first three empires.

The belief that this fourth empire would continue to the final coming of the Messiah, becoming partly iron and partly baked clay (two diverse materials which are unable to be fused together, thus creating deep inner tensions and stresses), is reinforced by a vision of John recorded in Revelation chapter 13. In that vision he saw a beast which was a composite creature resembling a leopard, but with the feet of a bear, and the mouth of a lion. It reveals that the 'world order' of the last days will be a joint-product of the character and culture of the Babylonian, Persian, Greek and Roman Empires (see Revelation 13:2; compare Daniel 7:2-28). In fact, the dream visions of the great statue described in Daniel chapter 2 and of the four beasts described in Daniel chapter 7 correspond, except that in the latter vision more emphasis is placed on the fourth kingdom and in particular the 'little horn' which arises out of it.

In the vision of Daniel chapter 8, the ram corresponds to the second part of the statue, the chest and arms of silver, and also to the second beast, the bear, both of which symbolize Persia. The he-goat corresponds to the third part of the statue, the belly and thighs of bronze, and also to the third beast, the leopard, both of which symbolize Greece (see Daniel 2:32, 39; 7:5,6). It is interesting to note the further emphasis upon 'a little horn'. In the vision of Daniel 7 it is identified as appearing at the end of the fourth kingdom, the Roman Empire (see Daniel 7:19-27), whilst in the vision of Daniel 8 it appears at the end of the Greek period. Its interpretation, in the latter chapter, it ought to be noted, is introduced specifically with the words, 'the vision concerns the appointed time of the end, (see Daniel 8:9-14, 23-25; compare verse 19).

Since the Greek period was not the conclusion of any divine phase or purpose, these words must mean that something more than that period is intimated. The revelation given by the angel in Daniel chapters 10 to 12 covers the same period as the he-goat of Daniel chapter 8, i.e. the Greek empire of Alexander the Great, and in particular, the continuous conflict and rivalry between the

Egyptian Ptolemaic kingdom of the south, and the Syrian Seleucid kingdom of the north, with an emphasis on a certain 'contemptible person' (*see* Daniel 11:21-12:4).

In my view it would be hard to dismiss a relationship between the prophecies of the 'little horn' of Daniel 8, the 'contemptible person' of Daniel 11, and the 'little horn' of Daniel 7. It would seem that in Daniel chapter 7 it is *the timing* of the antichrist's appearance which is in view; it is predicted for a time during the last period of modern civilization. In Daniel chapters 8 and 11 it is *the person* of the antichrist who is in view; it describes the Seleucid king, Antiochus IV Epiphanes, who, as the archtype of the 'man of sin', reveals many clues to his character, rule and policies.

To those who are unacquainted with biblical prophecy or these particular chapters in the book of Daniel the preceding paragraphs may appear complex and confusing. A prayerful study of such Scriptures, however, will yield much spiritual value to the child of God at any time, and may be of immense practical importance for the days ahead. As I have already stated, these prophecies have proved to be so remarkably accurate that it has made them suspect in the eyes of some scholars who consider that they have to be history written after the events described. Such accuracy must give us cause for strong confidence that what remains unfulfilled in the prophetic word will also be as accurately fulfilled. Furthermore, the subject takes on a new practical significance and meaning if the days in which we live are included in it.

If the 'times of the Gentiles' denote the domination and subjugation of the Jewish people by the Gentiles, those times should end with the emergence of a sovereign Jewish state. On 14th May, 1948 the state of Israel became a fact of modern history. The evidence that the times of the Gentiles have ended is found in the words of the Lord Jesus, 'Jerusalem will be trampled on by the Gentiles until the times of the Gentiles are fulfilled' (Luke 21:24). The plain meaning of his words is that the 'times of the Gentiles' will end when Jerusalem ceases to be subjugated and governed by Gentiles. Since the year A.D. 70, with the one exception of a few months in A.D. 135, Jerusalem has never been under sovereign Jewish government until 7th June 1967. Then the Israel Defence Forces recaptured the Old City and reunited Jerusalem to become 'the eternal and indivisible capital of Israel and of the Jewish people' as it was later proclaimed by an act of Knesset on 30th July, 1980. The times of the Gentiles have been fulfilled.

There are those Christians who are unable to accept that the words of Christ have such a meaning, and believe that the 'times of the Gentiles' and the 'fulness of the Gentiles' are synonomous. They understand his words to mean that Jerusalem will be trampled on by unbelieving Gentiles until the full number of the elect from among the Gentiles have been saved. In other words, they believe that Jerusalem will remain in the hands of the unsaved until the Messiah returns. It was, however, to the Jewish nation that Jesus spoke these words (*see* Luke 21:23). The immediate context makes it clear: as it was the Jewish people who would be dispersed worldwide and the Jewish capital which would be lost to them and taken over by the Gentiles, so it would be the Jewish people who would regain it in the future *when the times of the Gentiles would be fulfilled*.

If those times which commenced with the reign of King Nebuchadnezzar of Babylon were completed in 1967, then it has a vital and practical relevance for all who live in the latter part of the twentieth century. A long and important era of human history has ended and a new phase has begun which we who live in these days are privileged to witness. There are no explicit or concise indications in the prophetic word which would allow dogmatic assertions to be made concerning its duration but it must be comparatively short. The Scriptures call this phase 'the last days' or 'the time of the end' (*see* 2 Timothy 3:1; 2 Peter 3:3; Daniel 8:17, 19; 12:4). It could also be described as the threshold of the Messiah's coming (*see* Matthew 24:32-33). It will be characterized by Israel being at the centre of the world stage and the focal point of ferocious antagonism and battle; by a period of unparalleled shaking and change on every level of life; by the emergence of a 'world order' that will be increasingly antichrist in its social, moral, educational, political and religious concepts and attitudes; by a false and prostituted church, which will be a fusion of many religions and creeds, including all 'men of faith and good will', having a form of godliness without true spiritual content and power; by the appearance of a great 'saviour', the antichrist, who will head up this new order, and who will seek to destroy the true knowledge of God in the earth; and by the preparation of the redeemed people of God for the coming of the Messiah.

If a new phase of this age has begun, it will follow that it has many practical and spiritual implications for the people of God, both solemn and joyful. They are solemn because there will be new circumstances and conditions arising from change, upheaval, war, persecution, economic pressures, and national or international judgements by God. They are at the same time joyful because the prospect of being caught up to be with the Lord will approach steadily with each passing day.

Another lesson we learn from the book of Daniel is that God has been working out his purpose through world history from the beginning, and will continue to work it out until he has achieved his end. The space age of the twentieth century will neither hinder nor frustrate him. It is a mistaken belief that the Lord has limited himself to working only in the history of Israel and of the church and has left the nations to themselves, for 'the Most High God is sovereign over the kingdoms of men and sets over them anyone he wishes' (Daniel 5:21). He is the King of the universe, and the God of all flesh, even when he is not owned or recognized by nations or men. The history of the world is not some hopeless tangle of unrelated ends but is following a predestined course.

The rise and fall of empires, nations, ideologies, and great leaders is not haphazard but is ordained. This is true not only of ancient history but also of modern history. It is as true of the rise and fall of the Austro-Hungarian empire, the Turkish empire, the Nazi 'thousand year Reich' or the British empire as it is also of the rise and fall of the modern super-powers, the United States of America, and the Soviet Union, and of the appearance and disappearance of Capitalism and Marxism. They all come under the sovereign government of the King of the nations. Until the coming of the Messiah, God will continue to work all things according to the counsel of his will, not only through unsaved nations and their leaders, but even through the coming antichrist world order.

It was in the vision of world history given through the symbolism of wild beasts and culminating in an antichrist, that the Lord revealed to Daniel how it would end.

'... and there before me was one like a son of man, coming with the clouds of heaven. He approached the Ancient of Days and was led into his presence. He was given authority, glory and sovereign power; all peoples, nations and men of every language worshipped him. His dominion is an everlasting dominion that will not pass away, and his kingdom is one that will never be destroyed' (Daniel 7:13-14).

There is a further lesson from this outline of human history which God gave to Daniel that has real significance for every true believer. God reveals its true character by the two symbols which he uses to portray it: the symbol of a statue or an idol of a man; and the symbol

of savage beasts. In the dream which God gave to King
Nebuchadnezzar in Daniel chapter 2, he saw a huge statue
of a man, a colossus, or image. Nowhere is it suggested
that the idea of the ninety foot high image which King
Nebuchadnezzar set up to be worshipped in the next
chapter arose from this dream, but the association of the
two incidents seems obvious.

God's estimate of world history is that it is idolatry; it is
the story of man's self-worship and self-glorification,
often in the guise of religion. Its character is basically
humanistic and we see it coming to its fruition and full
manifestation in modern times. It is surely deeply significant that it is written, 'If anyone has insight let him
calculate the number of the beast, for it is man's number.
His number is 666' (Revelation 13:18). The history of
fallen man, whether it is the history of leaders, empires,
national interests or ideologies is the story of the worship
of man, and the dynamic which has so often driven
mankind to its greatest heights and its most depraved and
wicked depths has been the desire to glorify itself.

The apostle Paul made a most revealing statement
when he wrote, 'covetousness, which is idolatry' (Colossians 3:5) or, as it is translated in the NIV, 'greed, which
is idolatry'. Human history has been characterized by an
insatiable greed, or covetousness, on whatever level one
cares to investigate, and it has been the major cause of the
strife, wars, slavery, injustices, assassinations and mur-
ders which fill its pages.

A statue is impersonal and immobile. It may have a
magnificent and lifelike appearance but it has no heart or
life. World history provides evidence of many attempts to
provide mankind with a new and just order of society. In
theory they have appeared good and desirable, but in
practice they have proved to be impersonal, inflexible and
inhuman systems, often becoming monoliths of bondage
and despotism. They have no heart. Man always creates a

colossus which in turn enslaves him, then robs him of his individuality, originality and dignity, and, having reduced him to being no more than a cog in the economic or political machinery, ultimately destroys him. Heaven's answer to this travesty of God's plan for man is a divinely created rock which smashes the idol into pieces, and grows organically to fill the whole earth. God's new man, created in his own image and likeness through the finished work of the Lord Jesus, has both heart and life.

In the dream of Daniel recorded in chapter 7, human history is also portrayed by four savage beasts. They reveal the world's true character, hiding behind the statue's refined and sophisticated facade. Beneath the veneer of civilization with its vaunted ideals, education and social standards is the nature of a wild beast. The annals of human history provide abundant evidence for the bestiality of man's fallen nature, and its pages are filled with the stories of his savage butchery and inhuman cruelty. If this inhumanity could be relegated to ancient history and attributed to the ignorance and savagery of primeval man, the conscience of modern man could rest untroubled. He would be conscience-free, even if it could be attributed to pre-nineteenth century history and to man's slavery to bad social conditions or to bigoted prejudices. It is the opinion of the modern world that from all of this man has now evolved and been emancipated. But it is not the truth. The history of this century alone provides sufficient evidence of the continuing cruelty and wickedness of man. In fact, it would suggest that the bestiality of man is growing in intensity. The evidence for that is to be seen in the two world wars in which approximately 55,000,000 people died, apart from the many local and civil wars, ethnic strife, and terrorist atrocities perpetrated on innocent people during this century.

There are many examples from which one could draw,

but four give sufficient proof of the savage nature of world history in the twentieth century. The first example is the Turkish massacre of the Armenians (1915-1918) in which between 1,000,000 and 1,400,000 men, women and children were butchered in the most merciless and savage manner. This unusually gifted and artistic people were driven out of their homes for no other reason than that they were Armenians. Whether they were old, infirm, women, or children, they were sent on forced marches, which few survived, over hundred of miles of hostile country.

The second example is the Nazi liquidation of the Jews of Europe and Western Russia (1940-1944), in which at least 6,000,000 Jewish men, women and children died in the most horrific circumstances. Nothing in the pages of history could match the diabolical nature of the Nazis' 'final solution of the Jewish problem'. From the experimental operations performed upon people, without anaesthetics, to the bayoneting of one-month-old babes, it reveals an inhumanity without parallel. Even the remains of the gassed were utilized; human hair was used for upholstery, human flesh was melted down for soap, and human bones were ground into fertilizer.

The third example consists of the unnumbered millions who have died in Soviet prisons and forced labour camps, as a result of a deliberate state policy to reform or liquidate those who hold views different from those of the official party. It is a policy designed to break the minds and bodies of political prisoners, by means of the inhumane conditions imposed upon them, the heavy work quotas given to them, and the many forms of mental and physical torture to which they are subjected. It has been estimated that over the last fifty years, approximately 15,000,000 people have died in these circumstances, although some analysts place the figure much higher.

The last example is the deliberately planned liquidation

by the Khmer Rouge of a whole class of Kampuchean
(Cambodian) society in 1974, in which approximately
2,000,000 people died as a result of a de-urbanization
programme. The total population of cities and towns were
driven out into the countryside by armed men. This
included even those who had undergone recent surgery,
few of whom survived being removed from hospitals. It
was a policy aimed at the destruction of the professional
and educated classes, in order that a radical form of
Marxism might take root without opposition in the rest of
the population.

It must be a cause of deep concern for all thinking
people that mankind's progress is so superficial. In spite of
the long years of human history with its educational,
medical and social progress, with scientific knowledge and
expertise sufficient to send men to the moon and back,
contemporary man is as savagely cruel in nature, as
depraved in character, and as animal-like in behaviour, as
the worst of his forbears. Thousands of years ago, to an
old and godly Jewish statesman, wielding supreme authority in one of the greatest gentile empires known to
history, God portrayed the course of world history as four
wild beasts, of which the last was the most savage and
destructive.

For the redeemed of the Lord, the word of prophecy
reveals a truth which is cause for the most jubilant praise
and worship. The one who triumphs for ever over the
savagery and cruelty of the beast and all his works, and
over the dragon and all his works is a *lamb*! The difference
between the nature of a lamb and the nature of a wild
beast, or a dragon, needs no comment. It is the difference
between day and night, between light and darkness,
between heaven and hell, between the Christ and the
antichrist, and between God and Satan. God's 'lion of the
tribe of Judah, the root of David' is a 'lamb looking as if it
had been slain, standing in the centre of the throne of

God' (*see* Revelation 5:5,6). Throughout the last book of
the Bible we discover that it is the Lamb of God and the
followers of the Lamb, who triumph to reign for ever (*see*
Revelation 14:1-5; 19:6-7; 21:9-10; 22:1-5). The nature
and the character of the Lamb and his work is the rock
which strikes the image at its base and shatters it
completely, and then fills a renewed earth with his glory.
It is the Lamb of God who finally triumphs over the beast,
and realizes God's eternal purpose. The wickedness and
cruelty of the beast is only for time; it is the grace and the
glory of the Lamb which is eternal.

8. A land born in one day

If the times of the Gentiles have ended and a final phase of the age has commenced, however long it may last, it will be characterized by certain features. In this chapter we will consider one of those features: the state of Israel.

Israel is the divine time-clock of world history and by watching what is happening to the Jewish people, it is possible to determine what stage has been reached in the programme of God. She is the divine touchstone of world politics and the evidence that God is the God of history. Through her it is possible to see that there is an overall purpose and design in history. Those Christians who dismiss this subject as fanciful nonsense leave themselves without the means of spiritually determining the hour of the age, and, at the same time, rob themselves of an invaluable encouragement to faith.

No other nation has a history like the history of Israel: twice she has been exiled, and twice she has been regathered, the second exile lasting 1900 years and being a worldwide dispersal; twice she has lost her land and twice she has regained it; twice her national institutions and statehood have been destroyed and twice they have been restored; twice her capital, Jerusalem, has been taken away from her, and twice it has been returned to her. No other nation has had her language which, ceasing to be the common language of the people for at least 2,000 years and becoming a liturgical language for worship and Bible

study only, has suddenly been revived to become the
living language of a virile modern nation. And no other
nation has faced as many concerted attempts to liquidate
her and relegate her to a memory as Israel has faced
during her long history. Nevertheless they have all failed,
whether it has been the liquidation schemes of Pharaohs
or of the Nazis, or the more recent attempts of Islam.
From them all Israel has emerged more sound and lively
than she has ever been.

A century ago there was no Israel, and little likelihood
of her re-birth. It was easy at that time to dismiss the belief
in her eventual restoration as a nation to her land and
capital, Jerusalem, as representing an unbalanced and
superstitious approach to the Bible. Even forty years ago,
it would have seemed ridiculous to believe that the Jewish
people would ever again become a sovereign state, for
two-thirds of European Jewry were dying in the most
appalling circumstances. Today the nation of Israel is a
fact of history with her own president, her own leaders,
her own government, and her own well-trained and famed
army, airforce and navy. Remarkably and uniquely, as no
other small nation, she occupies a central place in world
affairs. Although her population numbers less than
4,000,000 people, her territory is no larger than Wales or
the State of Indiana, and her modern history spans a
period of only thirty-five years, she is endlessly discussed
in the capitals of the world, in world conferences, and
supremely at meetings of the United Nations Organization where she is the ground for multitudinous resolu-
tions, most of which are hostile in content. Every day she
is brought to world attention in newspapers, magazines,
on radio and television, so that there are few people on
earth who have not heard of the state of Israel. Only forty
years ago she did not exist; today she is a fact which it is
impossible to ignore!

If the preservation and existence of the Jewish people

today and the emergence of a sovereign Jewish state is a coincidence, it constitutes the most remarkable coincidence in history. When, however, the fact is faced that God has not only outlined the course of history in general but has predicted the history of the Jewish people in particular, we enter another dimension of the uniqueness of Israel. In countless prophecies the Lord has predicted the worldwide exile of the Jews, their long and unhappy sojourn among the nations, and their miraculous regathering to the promised land at the time of the end. The history of the Jewish people and of Israel reveals that God is behind world history working all things according to his own plan.

God predicted that they would return from the ends of the earth, from the north, the south, the east and the west; and they have returned from at least eighty-seven different nations, as far apart as New Zealand and Alaska or Chile and Afghanistan (*see* Isaiah 43:5-6; Jeremiah 31:7-9, 15-17). God predicted that they would rebuild the old cities and waste places, and plant orchards, vineyards and gardens; and they have rebuilt the ruined cities that have been devastated for generations, as the names of countless modern Israeli towns reveal, and have made the arid wilderness and malarial swamplands blossom as the rose (*see* Isaiah 61:4; Amos 9:14-15). God predicted that they would be fished out of the dispersion by fishermen, and hunted by hunters till they came back; and they were 'fished' back by the Balfour declaration of 1917, and 'hunted' back by the demonic hatred of the Nazis (*see* Jeremiah 16:14-16). God predicted that in one day their land would be born, and their nationhood would be brought forth; and so it happened on 14th May 1948 (*see* Isaiah 66:8). God predicted that their leaders would be one of their own, and their rulers would arise from among them; and today for the first time in 1900 years, the Jewish people are governed sovereignly by Jews (*see* Jeremiah

30:21). These prophecies are a sample of the many more that could be mentioned, and in my two previous books I have considered the subject more fully.

Some Christian leaders in the past, representing many different denominations, have confidently stated that there would *never* be a regathering of the Jewish people or the rebirth of the Jewish state, since God's purpose for them was concluded and they were rejected by him. Their statements to that effect in various Christian books and magazines could be cited. One would have thought that the emergence of the state of Israel in 1948, and its miraculous survival and triumph in spite of the unanimous verdict of the world's experts that it would be totally destroyed at birth, would have been the source of acute embarrassement to them, but it was not. On the contrary, they merely changed their tactics and facing the awkward fact as truthfully as they could, described it as a 'political accident'!

In my view, it would be impossible to study the Bible and to assert honestly that Israel has no divine destiny. To deny that destiny may solve the scriptural difficulties which some experience on this subject, but it raises far more serious and dangerous problems. A large number of prophecies have to be spiritualized in a subjective manner which may be of value, but it ignores their plain and original meaning; or they have to be interpreted as having been already fulfilled which may be partially true, but it either glosses over a number of glaring inaccuracies, or weakly explains them as the 'poetic licence' of the prophet. The result of this kind of approach is to undermine any confidence in the accuracy or the practical relevance of God's word. Another widely held view is that all these prophecies have been fulfilled in the church, the true Israel of God, and that there is, therefore, no future for the Jewish people. It then follows that it would be impossible for the state of Israel to be the fulfilment of

God's word and programme for world history, and that it must be the result of political manipulation and swindling on the part of the super-powers and the Jewish Agency, or, at the least, the result of their misguided ideals and energies.

It is my contention that altogether apart from the overwhelming Old Testament evidence, the New Testament reveals that God has neither irrevocably rejected his Jewish people, nor allowed them to stumble so as to fall beyond recovery (*see* Romans 11:1,11). Indeed, one would have to ignore the whole argument of Romans chapter 11 to conclude that the teaching of the New Testament rules out any future for the Jewish people. The apostle Paul stated the case lucidly when he wrote: 'But if their transgression means riches for the world, and their loss means riches for the Gentiles, how much greater riches will their fulness bring!' (Romans 11:12).

Christian and Jewish scholars are agreed that there was a national transgression and fall which led to political, territorial, as well as spiritual loss. The point made is not the fact that there was a transgression and a loss but that since their fall meant riches for the world, their *fulness* could only mean much greater riches! Furthermore, since the fall was national and spiritual; and since the loss was political, territorial, and spiritual, the fulness will also include all three of these elements. It is an unusual exegesis of God's word which takes only one half of a sentence and ignores the completion of it, especially when an important truth is at stake. To dwell on the transgression, the fall, and the loss of the Jewish people, and to ignore the promised fulness is not a right handling of the word of God. It is also as unacceptable to interpret the first part of the statement in national, territorial and spiritual terms and the last part in only personal and spiritual terms.

Paul returns to the theme in verse 15: 'For if their

rejection is the reconciliation of the world, what will their acceptance be but life from the dead?' There is little disagreement upon the question of the rejection, or 'casting away' of the Jewish people by God. It is generally recognized that it was comprehensive, involving them in the loss of their statehood, sovereignty, capital, land, economy, national temple and their spiritual standing. It is the *acceptance* of the same people which is often either by-passed or explained away in spite of the fact that in the same sentence their rejection is contrasted with their acceptance. It appears to me that as their fall and casting away began with their spiritual standing and ended with political and territorial matters, so their fulness and acceptance will be in reverse. It will begin with the restoration of their statehood, territory and capital, and will end with their salvation. In both these statements the main reference is to the abounding blessing, riches and resurrection life, which the restoration of the Jewish people will bring to the whole redeemed family of God.

Whatever opinion Christians may hold concerning the Jews, they have to admit that the Jews are 'the *natural* branches' of the olive tree, and those Gentiles who have been born of God's Spirit are the wild olive branches (*see* Romans 11:21,24; compare verses 17,19). The natural branches were broken off because of unbelief and the wild branches grafted in because of God-given faith; all the branches in this olive tree stand in it by faith. Once the unbelief of the natural branches has been replaced by living faith, they will much more easily be grafted into their own olive tree than were the wild branches.

It comes as a considerable shock to many Christians to realize that the true church of God is the Jewish people's 'own olive tree'. The apostle only speaks of one olive tree, and not two as some Christians assert. Their own olive tree (verse 24) is the same tree of which it is earlier stated,

'If the root is holy, so are the branches. If some of the branches have been broken off, and you, though a wild olive shoot, have been grafted in among the others and now share in the nourishing sap from the olive root, do not boast over those branches. If you do, consider this: You do not support the root, but the root supports you. You will say then, "Branches were broken off so that I could be grafted in." Granted. But they were broken off because of unbelief, and you stand by faith' (verses 16-20).

Christendom could be 'cut off' just as the Judaism of the first century was 'cut off' by the sternness of God, for it displays at this present time all those qualities which caused the fall of the Jewish people. No other people were more favoured and owned by God than the Jewish people. This sense of divine favour and care, however, fostered a pride and complacency which permitted many evils to nest within its branches; it produced an apathetic lukewarmness which allowed those cancerous evils to remain untouched, and a blindness which caused the day of their visitation to pass unrecognized, until judgement became inevitable. Christendom has arrived at the same place and displays the same character. Its attitude is most clearly expressed in the words of the Laodicean church, 'I am rich; I have acquired wealth, and do not need a thing' (Revelation 3:17). It is unable to recognize that in God's sight it is 'wretched, pitiful, poor, blind and naked' and that its Lord and Saviour has been banished to a place without, where he knocks upon its closed door to gain an entrance to that which owns his name and his word.

Inspired by the Holy Spirit, Paul wrote, 'Do not be arrogant, but be afraid. For if God did not spare the natural branches, *he will not spare you either.* Consider therefore the kindness and sternness of God: sternness to those who fell, but kindness to you, provided that you continue in his kindness. Otherwise, *you also will be cut off* ' (Romans 11:20-22, italics mine). The Lord Jesus could not have used a more strong or vivid term when he gave a similar warning to the Laodicean church in the words; 'So, because you are lukewarm – neither hot nor cold – I am about to spit you out of my mouth' (Revelation 3:16). The Greek word translated in the NIV 'to spit you out', or in the AV 'to spue thee out', means 'to vomit'. Christendom pontificates upon what it deems to be the past and present misdeeds and transgressions of the Jewish people, and particularly of the modern state of Israel. Yet it is apparently unable to recognize its own condition, or to hear the words of the risen Messiah, 'Be earnest and repent'.

It is important for a clear understanding of God's purpose for the Jewish people to note the words, 'Israel has experienced a hardening in part *until* the full number of the Gentiles has come in' (Romans 11:25, italics mine). There is no suggestion in these words that this 'hardening' is an unending judgement on the Jews. On the contrary, the word 'until' implies a time limit for it. The truth is that when the purpose of God to bring the Gentiles into the elect 'olive tree' has been concluded in principle, he will melt the 'hardening' which the Jewish people have experienced, with the most glorious results. Then multitudes of the natural branches will be grafted back into their own olive tree, and so all Israel will be saved, both the wild and the natural branches.

The ignorance of the Christian church concerning God's purpose for the Jewish people, and the debt she owes them, has given rise to many false concepts and teachings which in turn have unfluenced her attitudes and conduct toward the Jews. History might have been very different if she had only heeded the apostle's words, 'I do not want you to be ignorant of this mystery, brothers, so that you may *not be conceited* ...' (Romans 11:25, italics mine).

Many real Christians have no knowledge of the rela-

tionship of the Jewish people to the church of God. They
have no idea that all the writers of the New Testament
were Jewish with the possible exception of Luke; that all
the early apostles and leaders of the church were Jewish;
that the Messiah, Jesus, was Jewish, according to the
flesh, and had his *Brit mila* (his circumcision) on the
eighth day after his birth, and his *Bar mitzyah* (his coming
of age in the faith) when he reached his thirteenth
birthday; that every member of the body of Christ, the
church, was Jewish until the house meeting in Caesarea,
which launched her Gentile mission, the most successful
evangelistic mission ever undertaken by her. It has been
so successful that today the vast majority of Christ's
disciples have no knowledge of their Jewish origin, or of
the debt they owe to the Jews, or of the fact that the time
has arrived for the 'natural branches' to be grafted back
into their own olive tree. Apart from anything else, it
comes as a surprise to many Christians to be told that
some of their most famous cathedrals are named after
Messianic Jews. Consider for example St Peter's of
Rome, St Paul's of London, St Matthew's of New York,
St Mark's of Venice or St Stefan's of Vienna, to name only
a few of them.

It is all summed up in one sentence: 'As far as the
Gospel is concerned they are enemies on your account;
but as far as *election* is concerned, *they are loved* on
account of the patriarchs, *for God's gifts and his call are
irrevocable*' (Romans 11:28-29, italics mine). The simple
and dogmatic statement that God never withdraws or
cancels either his gifts or his call was made *in the first place*
concerning the Jewish people. They are enemies as far as
the Gospel is concerned, but are loved because of divine
election and grace. Nothing could be more clear than
these words. God has neither finally rejected his Jewish
people, nor hates or disdains them, but has shut up both
Jew and Gentile to disobedience that he might have mercy

on them all. The disobedience of the Jews has led the
Gentiles to the mercy of God. The same mercy, based
upon the finished work of the Messiah, which countless
Gentiles have experienced, will be the ultimate experience of countless Jews (*see* Romans 11:30-32). Then the
purpose of God to save both Jew and Gentile, which
began at Pentecost, will have come full circle.

9. The parable of the fig-tree

It is not only the inspired statements of the apostle Paul which furnish us with evidence for a restoration of the Jewish people, but also the clear statements of the Lord Jesus himself. After his last confrontation with the various parties which constituted the ruling classes of the nation at that time, Jesus uttered his most severe denunciation. He concluded it with the cry of his heart:

> 'O Jerusalem, Jerusalem, you who kill the prophets and stone those sent to you, how often I have longed to gather your children together, as a hen gathers her chicks under her wings, but *you were not willing*. Look, your house is left to you desolate. For I tell you, you will not see me again *until* you say, "Blessed is he who comes in the name of the Lord" ' (Mathew 23:37-39, italics mine).

Jesus' words betokened the most tragic period of Jewish history and her longest exile which began with the destruction of Jerusalem and the temple, and the world wide dispersal of the nation. There is, however, a clear time limit contained in the word 'until', and evidence of a radical change of heart on their part in the greeting, 'Blessed is he who comes in the name of the Lord'. In modern Hebrew, *baruch haba*, means 'welcome'; literally it means, 'blessed is he who comes'. For the people who were unwilling to obey his words, or to recognize his person and work, to utter such a welcome reveals a total change of attitude. These words of welcome for the returning Messiah are not the kind of words normally associated with those who are fleeing in terror of the coming judgement, but signify a work of grace which has produced a deep and saving recognition of him.

It was following that event that Jesus left the temple never to return to it. Descending into the Kidron valley, he crossed the brook, climbed the Mount of Olives and sat down with Peter, James, John and Andrew, somewhere on its slopes overlooking the whole of Jerusalem. They wanted to question him privately concerning the fulfilment of his words regarding the destruction of Jerusalem and the temple, and his coming and the end of the age. It became the occasion for a major discourse on his return recorded by all three synoptic Gospels: Matthew, Mark and Luke. Although in the minds of the disciples all their questions related to one final epoch of time, in fact the words of the Lord Jesus refer to two periods in the age. Its beginning marked by the destruction of Jerusalem and the fall of the nations, and its end, marked by the final events and his coming (*see* Matthew 24:1-3; Mark 13:1-4). He summed up the discourse by referring, in a striking way to the parable or lesson of the fig-tree.

'Now learn the parable from the fig tree: when its branch has already become tender, and puts forth its leaves, you know that the summer is near. Even so you too, when you see these things happening, recognize that He is near, right at the door' (Mark 13:28, 29 NASB; compare also Matthew 24:32, 33; Luke 21:29-31).

Is the lesson or parable of the fig-tree that as its bursting into leaf signals both the end of spring and the coming of the dry summer season, so the fulfilment of the signs which he has enumerated will signal his coming and the end of the age? It is a fact that the fig-tree is one of the last trees to break into leaf in Israel and heralds summer not spring. It is the almond tree, the first tree to blossom, which is the true harbinger of spring. The words of the Lord Jesus, 'when you see these things happening' (verse 29), would indicate that this is its lesson or parable.

But is that the *whole* lesson, or does it contain a further application that the Jewish people will be *the* sign of the last phase of world history and of the Messiah's return? The manner in which Luke records this statement is noteworthy; he writes, 'Look at the fig-tree *and all the trees*. When they sprout leaves, you can see for yourselves and know that summer is near'(Luke 21:29-30, italics mine). If Luke had wanted to correct any possible misunderstanding and make it clear that the fig-tree was not a symbol of the Jewish nation, as all the Jews of his day would have understood it to be, he could have written, 'Look at all the trees ...'. Instead Luke makes it clear, in my view, that the words of Christ have a twofold significance: 'all the trees' and 'the fig-tree'. There will be signs which will clearly warn that the time of the end is beginning, and a particular sign which will be *the* confirmation of it.

By New Testament times the fig-tree was already an established symbol of the land and the nation of Israel. It symbolized the physical fruitfulness of the national territory and the spiritual fruitfulness of the people (*see* Deuteronomy 8:8; I Kings 4:25; 2 Kings 18:31; Hosea 9:10; Zechariah 3:10). The phrase 'every man shall dwell under his own vine and fig-tree' should be noted, for it signified that every national would have an allotment of the promised land large enough to support a vine and a fig-tree. If no reference to Israel and the Jewish people was intended in this vitally important discourse, then the use of the fig-tree as a symbol only of coming summer was most unfortunate. It would have been less misleading to have used the symbol either of trees in general, or particular trees which had never symbolized the nation and its land. It is, however, in my view an inescapable conclusion that the Lord Jesus was referring to Israel.

It should not be overlooked that Mark chapters 11-13 cover a period of only two days. On the first of those days there had been an incident connected with a fig-tree which had made so deep an impression upon the disciples that on the next morning they had drawn the attention of Jesus to it (*see* Mark 11:13-14, 20). It was the occasion when Jesus had found no fruit on a fig-tree and had judged it. It is clear that it was an acted parable from the revealing comment 'because it was not the season for figs' (Mark 11:13). This acted parable should be compared with a spoken parable that Jesus had recounted earlier in his ministry in which he makes it clear that he used the fig-tree as a symbol of Israel.

> 'Then he told this parable: "A man had a fig-tree, planted in his vineyard, and he went to look for fruit on it, but did not find any. So he said to the man who took care of the vineyard, 'For three years now I've been coming to look for fruit on this fig-tree, and haven't found any. Cut it down! Why should it use up the soil?' 'Sir,' the man replied, 'leave it alone for one more year, and I'll dig round it and fertilise it. If it bears fruit next year, fine! If not, then cut it down' " ' (Luke 13:6-9).

For the three years of his public ministry, the Messiah had sought for fruit on the fig-tree but had found none. In the shadow of his cross, at the end of his public ministry and immediately before his final confrontation with the establishment of the nation, he acted out this parable on a fig-tree near Bethany (*see* Mark 11:15-18).

On the next morning his disciples had drawn his attention to it, for it had withered from its roots and in the late afternoon of that same day he had said to them, 'From the fig-tree, learn its parable' or 'its lesson'. It is clear that all four disciples must have had that fig-tree in mind, and even if they had not connected the events of the previous two days with it, after Pentecost they would certainly have understood the connection.

The parable of the fig-tree contains a twofold lesson relating in general to the signs which will usher in his coming and in particular to the Jewish people: their land, their statehood, and their destiny. The meaning of the first lesson is self-explanatory, but what of the second? It is that the Jewish people would never disappear or be destroyed. Even though the nation was withering from its roots because of unbelief and transgression, and would experience the loss of everything in a second exile, worldwide in its extent, and unparalleled in its sorrow, at the appointed time they would re-emerge as a nation. They would regain their statehood, their land, and their capital, and this restoration would be as miraculous as a tree which had died from its roots, and which had long been obviously dead, reviving to become a healthy, vigorous, and fruitful tree. It would, therefore, be entirely unwarranted to draw the conclusion, that the fall and the loss of the nation was a final and irrevocable judgement by God. At the end of the age, the same nation would be present, and not merely alive but virile, and full of the promise of fruit.

The relevance of the parable of the fig-tree for the people of God is that when all these things begin to happen, and in particular, when the Jewish state re-emerges from its long death, they would be able to recognize that 'He is near, right at the door' (Mark 13:29 NASB). The phase which could be described as the *threshold* of the Messiah's return would have arrived. Simply stated this means that the rebirth of the state of Israel on 14th May 1948 is a prophetic milestone. Many of the signs which the Lord Jesus had predicted such as, for instance, wars, rumours of wars, earthquakes, famines (whether of food, energy, natural resources, or basic raw materials), or the persecution of believers could have been validly applied to other eras of this age. All of them have been either the continuous experience of mankind or have marked particular periods of history. It is possible, therefore, to understand previous generations of believers who considered that the troubles of their day were unique and were a possible fulfilment of those signs, especially if the one sign which was intended to validate the rest was not rightly understood. Nevertheless it should be clear that to be *obvious* beacons of the last days, those signs would have to be worldwide and unusually intense in nature. It is also as important to understand that *the* sign which would guard against any misinterpretation of current world events would be the re-emergence of the Jewish state. It is an unchallengeable fact that the only sign which could not have been applied to any other part of this age, except the last generation, is the rebirth of Israel.

The history of Israel contains many apparent 'coincidences' which in my estimation reveal the hand of God. They range from the total destruction of Jerusalem by Nebuchadnezzar on the 9th Av (July-August) in 587 B.C. and again by Titus on the exact same day in A.D. 70, both of which marked the beginning of an exile for the Jews, to the death of the Messiah, the Lord Jesus, as the Lamb of God, during Passover in A.D. 30, when the Passover lambs were sacrificed, and the meal was eaten in commemoration of God's redemption from Egypt.

The recent history of Israel also contains such apparent 'coincidences'. In September 1897, for example, at the first Zionist Congress held in the Stadt Casino, Basel, in Switzerland, which incidentally was also the first worldwide gathering of Jewish leaders since the Sanhedrin was disbanded, Theodor Herzl noted in his diary: 'If I were to sum up the Basel Congress in a few words – which I would not dare to make public – I would say, "At Basel, I founded the Jewish state!" If I said this aloud, it would be greeted with worldwide derision. In five years, perhaps, and certainly in fifty, everyone will see it' (*The Diaries of Theodor Herzl*, edited by Marvin Lowenthal, London, 1958, page 224). His prediction was fulfilled in exactly fifty years, for in November 1947, the United Nation General Assembly passed a resolution, by a two-thirds majority, calling for the establishment of a Jewish state. Those fifty years were to prove the most turbulent years in the long, turbulent history of the Jewish people. They had begun with the adoption of a national flag and a national anthem but without a state, or a land, and were to end, in spite of the Nazi era, in the establishment of Israel. The word of God speaks of the Year of Jubilee, the fiftieth year, in which all property reverts to its rightful owner (*see* for example Leviticus 27:24; compare Leviticus 25:9-55). Was it a coincidence or was it by divine design that in the Jubilee Year that which had commenced with only a national claim and aspiration based upon the Bible finished as a reborn nation in its own land?

It was on 11th December 1917 that General Edmund Allenby walked bareheaded through the jubilant crowds into the old city of Jerusalem to proclaim officially from the steps of the Citadel of David her liberation from seven hundred years of Islamic domination. The Turks had actually surrendered on 9th December. The 11th December happened to be the first day of Hanukkah, the Jewish Festival of lights and freedom, which celebrates the miraculous Maccabean triumph over the cruel Seleucid conquerors in the second century B.C., a triumph which marked a new era of national glory.

The previous month had witnessed yet another historic milestone of immense significance to the Jewish people, the Balfour Declaration of 2nd November 1917, in which the British Government declared that it '... favoured the establishment in Palestine of a national home for the Jewish people ...'. Fifty years later on 7th June 1967, the old city of Jerusalem was recaptured in a lightning move of the Israel Defence Forces and reunited with West Jerusalem, to be proclaimed 'the eternal and indivisible capital of Israel and the Jewish People'. Was it coincidence or was it by divine design that it was the Jubilee Year, the fiftieth year in which property should return to its rightful owner, that Jerusalem was restored to the Jewish people; or that in a war forced upon her by her neighbours she emerged victorious and in possession of much more of the promised land?

On 6th October 1973, on the holiest day of the Jewish calendar, the Day of Atonement, a war was suddenly and simultaneously launched on two fronts on Israel. It was a war she could have easily lost, but which, miraculously she not only survived but won. Was it a coincidence, or was it by divine design that it began on that day? In my view, it was not a coincidence. Its commencement on Yom Kippur has solemn significance, and is a further milestone in the programme of God, marking the beginning of the build-up for the war described in Ezekiel chapters 38 and 39. The fact that since 1973 Syria and the Soviet Union have signed a defence pact; that Syria has become a huge Soviet arsenal in the Middle East; that Iran (Persia) has changed from being Israel's friend to her sworn enemy; and that both Ethiopia and Libya are more hostile to her than at any previous time only confirms my view that we are in the run-up to a third world war with the most serious consequences for the whole world, and particularly for Western Europe. The added fact that there is a race to obtain a nuclear capability on the part of Islamic nations, in particular Pakistan, Iraq and Libya, all of which are bitterly hostile to Israel, is a further confirmation. It was only the Israeli precision bombing of the Baghdad nuclear plant which hindered Iraq from winning that race. On the wider horizon, there is a slowly deteriorating world situation evidenced by the events in

Afghanistan, Poland and Central America. If the pre-1973 world was a difficult place in which to live, the post-1973 world is much more difficult, with its spiralling inflation and economic recessions, its energy shortages, its oil weapon blackmail, its anarchy and lawlessness, and its violent terrorism.

The war predicted by Ezekiel would in all likelihood see the destruction of the Soviet monolith, and the end of Marxism as it has been known; the liberation of Russia and of China; and the serious crippling of the power of Islam. The true church of God could then be presented with a short period of political, economic, and moral vacuum in the world, offering the greatest opportunities for the Gospel which she has had since Pentecost. That period would end with the rise of the antichrist and the last events of the age. If what I have written is true, it follows that it is of vital importance that God's people wake up and begin to prepare for such a period of opportunity.

The Yom Kippur war also marked the public manifestation of that demonic principality which has energized the current Islamic revival. That revival is apparent throughout the Muslim world from the Philippines and Malaysia in South-East Asia to Mauretania and Senegal on the Atlantic coast of North West Africa. His activity is most clearly expressed in the Iranian Islamic Revolution, under the leadership of the Ayatollah Khomeini, with all its cruelty and bloodshed, as well as in the rapid growth of the fanatical Moslem Brotherhood in most of the Islamic nations. It is a spirit from hell which has arisen, as strong as the spirit which energized the Bolshevik Revolution of 1917, or the Nazi triumph of 1933, and it will cause much blood to be shed before it is destroyed.

Christians who think that Islam is a 'sister religion' of Judaism and Christianity, worshipping the one god, and sharing the same basic ideals, are deceived. Any true servant of God who has worked for a length of time in an

Islamic country should be able to enlighten such Christians. It is a fact that the same serious difficulty in being born of the Spirit is experienced by spiritists or by persons involved in occult practice and by Muslims. There is a demonic bondage which first has to be broken in the name of Jesus before they are able to taste God's saving grace.

Islam is a triumphalist religion. It believes that it is God's final word and his ultimate revelation to man, and of necessity has to conquer the whole world; the word *Islam* means submission. It proclaims that what God began with the Jews, and developed with the Christians, he fulfilled with Mahommed. It states that both Jews and Christians tampered with the Scriptures to serve their own ends but the Koran has corrected them and is the true word of God. It recognizes all the patriarchs and prophets of the Bible as its own, including Jesus, who was the Messiah, was born of a virgin and was crucified, but who did not die an atoning death, because God spirited him away. It believes that he ascended and will return but vehemently denies that he is the Son of God. This last Koranic declaration appears twice on the frieze around the Dome of the Rock which stands on the temple site in Jerusalem. It is interesting to note that Islam denies the heart of the Gospel. It denies the sonship of the Lord Jesus, his atoning death and his bodily resurrection.

It is important for Christians to recognize that inherent in Islam is the fanatical belief that it has to triumph worldwide. If Jews or Christians will neither disparage nor contend with its basic tenets of belief as revealed in the Koran, they are accorded special status in its eyes as 'people of the book'. If they are unable to accept that Mahommed is *the* prophet, or that Islam is *the* true way, and speak against it, they are worthy only of death. If they are spineless and without living faith or experience they will be acceptable, but it they are on fire for their faith they will collide with Islam and will have to be destroyed.

The spread of Islam was so dynamic that within a century of its beginnings, by means of the *Jihad*, or holy war, it had reached eastwards to all of Central Asia and to India, and westwards to Spain, conquering everything in its way. Its triumphant progress in Europe was only halted, by the grace of God, at the Battle of Poitiers in A.D. 732, two hundred miles from Paris. It retired defeated to Spain, from which it was finally expelled in A.D. 1492. In its second attempt to take the world under the Ottoman Turks, it reached as far as the heartlands of Europe and only came to a halt at the battle of Vienna in A.D. 1683. It is a considerable shock for some believers to realize how near Europe and Britain came to Islamic conversion. After this defeat it retired to stagnate slowly over the centuries until the discovery in the twentieth century of its oil resources.

Muslim leaders faithful to Islam believe that *Allah* has given them oil, and the immense wealth which has accrued from it, in order that Islam might finally conquer the world. What could not be won through the sword, will be won through the weapon of oil, gold, and economic pressure. The goal remains the same, the subjugation of the world to Islam. It is hard for some Christians to realize that Islam is not a decayed, spineless, and benevolent eastern religion, but a militant threat to both Judaism and Christianity as real as militant Marxism. It will only tolerate Jews and Christians if they will come to terms with it as a conqueror, and the virile Islam which is in evidence in Iran and Libya, intends to eliminate all opposition to its authority and sovereignty. It is a mistake of the first magnitude to believe that Islam's only contention is with Israel and the Jews; it is also with the church and the Christian.

It is this which lies at the root of the whole battle over Israel, for if Islam is the final word of God the rebirth of a Jewish state is an impossibility, and its survival and

triumph an obscence affront to it. Individual Jews or
Jewish communities could be tolerated as the antique
remnants of a nation which God once honoured, but a
modern Jewish state and nation explodes the Islamic
contention that the Jews are disowned by God, and that
Islam is their successor and fulfilment. The very existence
of Israel poses a continous threat to her faith and claims
and explains the vehement hatred shown toward her. By
its nature, therefore, it is unable to accept a Jewish state,
and if it has to recognize her, it will *only be with a view to
her final destruction at a more opportune time*.

For this reason Jerusalem lies at the centre of this
conflict and will be the flashpoint of contention until Islam
falls (*see* Zechariah, chapters 12 and 14). Although
Jerusalem ranks in Muslim eyes only as the third most
holy city, Mecca and Medina both taking priority over
her, and is not mentioned even once by name in the
Koran, it would be impossible for Islam to recognize
Jerusalem as the capital of a Jewish state. To recognize
her as such would be to acknowledge defeat by that which
itself should have long before disappeared in defeat! It is
not without significance that the main source of this
contention is the temple area in Jerusalem containing the
Dome of the Rock, which Christians of previous generations considered to be 'the abomination of desolation' and
the Mosque of El-Aksa which stands upon the site of
Solomon's porches where the early church gathered
together to pray and to worship.

Governments of the United States of America and
Western European nations and even Christians who
consider that the continuous strife in the Middle East is
the result of mere politics, economics, or gross nationalism, have misunderstood the situation. The real situation
is spiritual and theological; it is an ideological confrontation. For what possible reason could the Islamic nations,
with their vast territories, their large rivers, and their

immense oil resources and wealth, want Israel, a land which is no larger than Wales, and is devoid of such resources, unless the reason was spiritual? It is hard for westerners who live in a society in which religion and theology have been devalued to a sentimental and traditional observance of little consequence in national life and policy, to believe that it could play a dynamic role in the space age. But that is the role it plays in many Islamic nations.

Furthermore, this explains the recent sad history of the Lebanon, in which even before the most recent troubles, at least 70,000 people died in the last decade. The Lebanon was the only Christian Arab state in the Middle East, and the centre of all Arabic Gospel work. There is little doubt that it has been the destruction of her Christian character which has guided the Islamic nations in their handling of her problems. Even if this was not their deliberate policy, it has been the practical result of it, for it has been the aim of the demonic being who has inspired the Islamic revival and revolution to destroy any true Christian witness in Arab lands.

Israel, and Jerusalem in particular, are destined to be the cause of much more conflict and war in the future. There is no need to fear the outcome; Israel will not only survive, she will triumph. She will neither be dismembered, nor will she be destroyed. It will be all those nations and ideologies which pit themselves against her, which will be broken, and broken because of her. It will make no difference whether they are super-powers, or alliances of powerful nations, or political or religious ideologies which are entrenched and worldwide. They will fall every one. God's purpose is to use Israel in a world increasingly alienated from him and his word to reveal that there are spiritual principles involved in her existence. Stage by stage the world will be forced to recognize that Israel's survival and triumph is not due to her own native genius, wealth, or military prowess, but to God. In the end, although restored to her statehood, her land and her capital in blindness, her Messiah will reveal his identity to her. Then the hardening which Israel has experienced will melt away, and she will be granted radiantly clear vision resulting in salvation. This will be the last piece of evidence that God will place before the nations that Jesus is the Messiah, the Son of the Living God (*see* for example Zechariah 12:10-14; Ezekiel 39:21-29). Then the nations will know that it was God who exiled Israel and who restored her, who rules over the history of the nations and works all things according to his will. The Holy One of Israel, her persistent Guardian and Lover, will finally reveal himself as her everlasting Redeemer.

10. The great shaking

A further feature which will characterize the time of the end will be a shaking of the heavens and the earth, unparalleled in the long history of man. We find this promised in the letter to the Hebrews in the words:

'See to it that you do not refuse him who speaks. If they did not escape when they refused him who warned them on earth, how much less will we, if we turn away from him who warns us from heaven? At that time his voice shook the earth, but now he has promised, "Once more I will shake not only the earth but also the heavens." The words "once more" indicate the removing of what can be shaken – that is, created things – so that what cannot be shaken may remain' (Hebrews 12:25-27).

It is possible to gain much value from spiritualizing this shaking as a period of immense and universal change and upheaval in the political, economic and moral spheres of life. Nevertheless, it is clear that *in the first place* it predicts a physical shaking of the earth and the heavens, catastrophic in its consequences, and mercifully cut short by the Messiah's return.

All the synoptic Gospels bear witness to this truth. In the Gospel of Luke the words of the Messiah are recorded, 'There will be signs in the sun, moon and stars. On the earth, nations will be in anguish and perplexity at the roaring and tossing of the sea. Men will faint from

terror, apprehensive of what is coming on the world, for
the heavenly bodies will be shaken. At that time they will
see the Son of Man coming in a cloud with power and
great glory' (Luke 21:25-27). Both the Gospels of Matthew and Mark record more fully what he said concerning
the sun, moon and stars: 'Immediately after the distress of
those days, the sun will be darkened, and the moon will
not give its light; the stars will fall from the sky, and the
heavenly bodies will be shaken. At that time the Son of
Man will appear ...' (Matthew 24:29-30; compare Mark
13:24-25; Isaiah 13:6; 34:4).

Joel's prophecy also predicted that such signs would
usher in the day of the Lord. The apostle Peter in his
message on the day of Pentecost spoke of Joel's words as
being fulfilled in the pouring out of the Holy Spirit and the
beginning of the New Testament age. It is also as clear
that they are to mark the development and the end of the
age because of the concluding statement: 'I will show
wonders in the heaven above and signs on the earth
below, *blood and fire and billows of smoke. The sun will
be turned to darkness and the moon to blood before the
coming of the great and glorious day of the Lord.* And
everyone who calls on the name of the Lord will be saved'
(Acts 2:19-21; compare Joel 2:30-31, italics mine). This
theme of the sun and the moon being darkened, the stars
falling from their course, or ceasing to shine, and
earthquakes or other physical phenomena on the earth,
reoccurs in many prophecies concerning judgement and
the end of this world's history (*see* for example Joel 2:10;
3:15-16; Ezekiel 32:7-8; Revelation 6:12-13; 8:12).

It is important to note two things concerning this
shaking. Firstly, it will characterize the very end of the last
days; both Matthew and Mark prophesy that it will follow
a period of distress and tribulation and immediately
precede the return of the Messiah; Luke prophesies that it
will follow the end of the times of the Gentiles and usher

in the Lord's coming; and Joel prophesies that it will immediately precede 'the coming of the great and glorious day of the Lord'. And secondly, a number of these signs could be inter-related in action; for example, a darkening of the sun would automatically affect the light of the moon, which in turn could affect the tides of the seas, the weather, the seasons and life itself.

Nothing could be more skilfully designed to shake man's faith in himself and in his wisdom and ability than such disturbances in this planet and its universe. Although man is often shocked at his own ability, through war, revolution or anarchy, to overthrow and destroy the structure and standards of normal life, he is generally able to cope with it, since the disorder is 'man-made' and he can understand it. Serious problems in the sun, the moon, the stars, or the oceans and tides, such as those forecast in the Bible, are beyond his ability either to understand or to solve. He is unable to cope with them in spite of the great technological knowledge and expertise of the space age. Hence the words recorded by Luke: 'Men will faint from terror, apprehensive of what is coming on the world, for the heavenly bodies will be shaken' (Luke 21:26).

It is apparent from the words of the Lord Jesus that this physical shaking of the universe is the final stage in a shaking of every aspect of human life whether political, economic, educational, religious, social, moral or spiritual (see Matthew 24:4-14; Mark 13:5-13; Luke 21:8-19). He spoke of wars, rumours of wars, and violent antagonism between nations; of revolutions; of earthquakes, famines or shortages, and plague diseases; and of the persecution of his disciples. Each of these alone would normally shake human society, but he prophesied that, at the beginning of the end, they would be combined in an ever-growing intensity and pressure. These are all features which disrupt normal life, destabilizing society and producing disorder, discontent and unhappiness; they become catalysts for violent change whether for good or for evil. When combined, these constituents produce a recipe which is designed to shake to pieces anything which is not eternal. The child of God should never forget that it is not the powers of darkness but the Lord who has created the recipe. The Lord merely uses satanic forces as ingredients.

The Messiah expressly spoke of this shaking as marking not the end, but the *beginning* of the end. Indeed, for the encouragement of his disciples, he described it in the most vivid and positive terms as 'the beginning of birth pangs' which would end in his coming and the arrival of his kingdom (*see* Matthew 24:6,8; Mark 13:7-8; Luke 21:9). This period of progressive shaking, ever growing more violent, will evolve into a comparatively short era of time in which the antichrist will appear as the world's saviour and deliverer from war and disorder, and her prince of peace. His meteoric rise to power will be owed in no small measure to the upheavals and disorder of this century. The last part of his rule will be marked by a time of tribulation more severe than anything which has preceded it (*see* Matthew 24:15-28; Mark 13:14-23).

This period of upheaval and tumultuous change began, in my view, with the First World War of 1914-18. It was a war which no one really wanted, or so historians inform us, and which few of the main actors in the drama expected. In spite of that it happened as if all the participants were the slaves of fate and circumstances, locked into a battle which was ultimately to destroy them. It was the beginning of a shaking which was to shatter a whole way of life and society. The Second World War is often thought to have been the real catalyst of change in this century, but it merely finished that which began with the First World War. With its conclusion, a whole way of life, which over the centuries had suffered little substantial change, had disappeared. At that stage few realized what was happening; the full extent of it only became clear with the passage of time. Empires and thrones had disappeared never to reappear: the Austro-Hungarian Empire and its Emperors; the Ottoman Empire and its Sultans; the Russian Empire and its Czars; the German Kingdom and its Kaisers; and immediately preceding the war in 1914, the Chinese Empire and its Emperors. These empires, kingdoms, and thrones had, in some instances, been in existence for a thousand years, but in four years they were all swept away.

It was an era of unparalleled turmoil for civilization. Marxism came of age in 1917 in the midst of that upheaval and emerged to dominate mankind for the rest of the century until today. There is no doubt that the warring powers of Europe would have rushed to the support of the Czar, if they had not been locked in battle with each other, and would have crushed the Bolshevik Revolution at its birth. But with the flower of European and British manhood dead, the battle-weary nations could send only token forces to Russia, and Bolshevism triumphed. Those years of turmoil and upheaval were to lead to another birth with the Balfour Declaration of November 1917 and with the liberation of Jerusalem from 400 years of Ottoman rule in December 1917. In was the birth of a Jewish State. From all the changes produced by that war, men and women emerged with new attitudes to life. There was a great falling away from the churches, and a growth of secularism, agnosticism and atheism; the beginnings of a new outlook on marriage, divorce, the family, and sexual purity; and the rise of intellectual and political movements which had as their aim the destruction of the Judeo-Christian norms of living and their replacement with earlier pagan norms. It required, however, a Second World War to set in motion those forces which would not only cause these new attitudes to gain general acceptance, but also to introduce far more radical concepts and ideas.

The Second World War of 1939-45 involved many more nations and covered much more territory than the First World War. It was horrific in its suffering because of the new and more deadly weapons used, the immense scale of fighting, and the manner in which civilian populations were involved. An estimated 55,000,000 people died during its course, 20,000,000 of them in concentration camps in Europe and the Far East. It marked the beginning of the atomic age with the explosion of an atom bomb on the Japanese city of Hiroshima, resulting in its instantaneous destruction and the incineration of 100,000 people. From that time the world has witnessed the creation of ever more powerful nuclear weapons capable of destroying all life and of blowing apart the planet itself.

It led to the disappearance of the British Empire and its hardly recognizable reappearance as the British commonwealth of nations. It also led to the end of the colonialism of the Western powers with the resulting emergence of so many new states that the political map of the world has entirely changed, and is still changing. In the midst of all this turmoil, and in spite of the fact that at least a third of her people had been liquidated, Israel was reborn to take her place in the roll call of the world's sovereign states.

Until this war, Marxism had been confined to the Soviet Union, or to small revolutionary forces of rebels fighting within other countries. It had not gained control of any other land. From that time, however, it emerged as a world force with half of Europe in its iron-like grip. It was destined to conquer many nations, until half the world's population has come under its control. It has been a major constituent in the shaking for few forces in history have caused such violent change and suffering as has communism.

The shaking did not cease with the conclusion of that war, but has grown in violence and intensity, until the present world would be almost unrecognizable to the pre-1914 world. The political, economic and moral changes which began with the First World War, and which were powerfully advanced by the Second World War, have speeded up since then. In all probability it will take another world war to bring those changes to completion in a new world order, in a world government and police force, in a false world church, and in a new morality for the desired 'new age'.

The new attitude to life and society with which the nations emerged from the Second World War was based substantially on the Darwinian and Marxist view of man as evolving from matter, as no more than a highly intelligent and noble animal. It was no longer founded on the revealed truth that man was made in the image and likeness of God, and is, therefore, accountable to God. It follows, therefore, that if man is an animal, the Judeo-Christian concepts of man, of sex, of marriage, of the family, and of society, should be reconsidered since they have to be largely, if not totally, erroneous. They must be reconsidered even if such concepts have had their value in past centuries and may still have a 'mystical' value. In this view, they are identified as the cause of much unnecessary psychological illness and problem, giving rise to an unhealthy conscience and to damaging inhibitions in the individual, as well as in society. It has led to a revolution in the whole concept of sex; to a popular acceptance of the legitimacy of sex before marriage, which has been greatly aided by the new and easy forms of birth control; to a serious weakening of the sanctity of marriage, and an enormous increase in divorce; to the legalization of homosexuality; and the general acceptance of much lower standards regarding pornography. It has also led to the legalization of abortion, since man is viewed as an animal, and therefore as expendable as an unwanted animal; and to an atmosphere in which the legalization of euthanasia, or so-called 'mercy killing', would be possible.

The violent and inhuman terrorism, which has burst upon the world in these last decades, is also largely based on this concept of man. It is a philosophy of violence and lawlessness, which allows innocent people to be used as pawns in a game of chess. They may be murdered, if necessary, without any conscience, since 'the end justifies the means', and man is expendable. Outrages have been perpretrated upon innocent people in order to spread fear and cause the disruption of society, or simply as a means of gaining publicity for a terrorist cause, or because they represent a hated society which the terrorist wishes to overthrow. This brutality and carnage is justified in the eyes of the terrorist since it is in the interests of some higher good for mankind. It is no small paradox that deeds of unimaginable wickedness are performed by idealistic young men and women possessed by a vision of a new and good society. The growth of this kind of terrorism has been so phenomenal and its operations have become so commonplace that the general public has become almost hardened to it. It is a sad fact that the governments of the western democracies have proved to be so spineless in their handling of the problem. They will take any action to appease the terrorists, or will compromise themselves in secret agreements in order to avoid any operations or confrontations with them in their domains. They have truly become a mixture of the 'iron' of authority, and the 'baked clay' of weakness. It is the beginning of the 'lawlessness' which the prophetic word predicts as the hallmark of the last phase of world history, and of which the antichrist will be the great propagandist and hero (*see* 2 Thessalonians 2:1-12). International terrorism is yet another constitutent of the shaking.

The phenomenon of the Islamic revival in the past decade is a further constitutent, and there is no part of the Islamic world which has not been touched by it. Those who remember the Nazi era will have had strange feelings as they witnessed the mass rallies and euphoria of the Iranian Islamic revolution and watched its main personality, the Ayatollah Khomeini, for he is as demonically inspired as were Hitler and the Nazis. That revival and revolution is intended for export throughout the Muslim world and beyond it to the non-Muslim world, and is a major cause of unrest wherever there are nations with sizeable Muslim populations. A further source of unrest is Libya's inspiration of everything which is radical in the Arab world, its designs on Muslim black Africa, and its immense ideological and practical support for many forms of international terrorism. Furthermore, the fact that a sizeable portion of the world's wealth as well as much of the free world's oil supplies are in Muslim hands only adds to the strength and influence of Islam.

Since 1973 there has been a growing shaking of the world's economy with spiralling inflation, recessions, and resulting unemployment. Always on the horizon, there has been the haunting spectre of a world-wide depression and monetary collapse. To these facts we have to add the further facts of a huge population explosion, predicted shortages of food, energy, and raw materials, and the growing pollution of the world's natural assets, particularly of the air and of the seas. These facts present the modern world with no small problem or danger but she has the resources and the ingenuity to face them and overcome them. If, however, there were to be any combination, for example, of serious war, revolution in strategic areas, physical disturbances in the universe resulting in the disturbing of climatic conditions and the disruption of normal life, or plague diseases, the effect would be disastrous. It is exactly this kind of combination of circumstances and events which the Lord Jesus predicted.

Every true disciple, therefore, needs to consider carefully the words of the Messiah: 'when these things *begin* to take place, stand up and lift up your heads, because *your redemption is drawing near*' (Luke 21:28, italics mine). These words were given for our faith, encouragement and strengthening in one of the most difficult phases of human history. There is no need to fear since, by the grace of God, we are on the winning and unshakeable side in this conflict. 'We are receiving a kingdom that cannot be shaken' (Hebrews 12:28). Our paramount need is to discover the nature and the life of its invincible king so that we may not be shaken but be enabled to overcome. There is no valid reason to panic, or to be fearful. Even if the believer were to lose his physical life because of his faithfulness to the Lord, not one hair of his head will perish, but in a miracle of redemptive power, his whole body will be restored in glorious life. The one who has been saved by God, and is faithful to God, is unable to lose!

We are moving steadily into an era of ever growing change and turmoil. It is an era in which the basic foundation and structure of civilised society is being challenged on every level, whether political, economic, religious or moral. The issue at stake is whether that society should be governed by the 'rule of law' or by 'lawlessness'.

It is important that Christians should understand that this is not merely a challenging of man-made laws and statutes, but also of the basic law of God. It is a determined onslaught on God's word as revealed truth, and constitutes the most serious challenge yet issued by the forces of darkness and evil in this age. Its aim is the overthrow of God's word and its replacement with new 'truth', ideals and standards for a new age.

For Christians living in a society in which every aspect of life is increasingly related, it presents complex problems. To stand apart from the new trends of thought, or from officially accepted new standards, causes them to appear old-fashioned, unhealthy and narrow-minded. Take for example the world of education where the battle for the soul of nations is being fought. Young Christians, whether at school, college or university, are increasingly exposed not only to an atmosphere which is pagan, but also to basic premises of teaching which are anti-Christian. The same problem has to be faced in the medical, scientific or commercial world, as in the whole area of social work, where the ethical principles and standards governing conduct and practice are no longer Judeo-Christian but pagan. If in the past, it was difficult to remain uncompromised and faithful to the Lord in these areas of national life, it will become infinitely more difficult as time progresses.

The revelation of the word of prophecy that a shaking will characterize the end times is, therefore, of great practical relevance for the people of God today. A right understanding of it will not only preserve them from being taken unawares by the shaking, but will explain its purpose, and will enable them to pass through it with eternal gain. God designs through it to shake to pieces everything which is not of himself, everything which can be shaken in order that as many people as possible may discover that which is eternal and unshakeable. Christians are neither excluded from this shaking, nor are they automatically immune to it. If they have not dug deeply and laid their foundations upon the rock, the whole superstructure of their faith and life is liable to be shaken down (see Luke 6:46-49). If, however, they have laid their foundations upon the rock which is Christ himself, and not upon the topsoil of their own natural energies, second-hand experience or cultural background, they have nothing to fear. There is no storm, or flood, capable of destroying him or those who are in him. If our treasure is in the right place, we will have little to lose, and everything to gain. We shall discover the unshakeable and invincible nature of God's city, and the river of life and power which supplies it throughout the upheaval and change. With the Psalmist we shall be able to declare:

> God is our refuge and strength,
> A very present help in trouble.
> Therefore will we not fear,
> Though the earth do change,
> And though the mountains be moved
>   in the heart of the seas;
> Though the waters thereof roar and be troubled,
> Though the mountains shake with
>   the swelling thereof.
>
> There is a river, the streams whereof
>   make glad the city of God,
> The holy place of the tabernacles of the Most High.
> God is in the midst of her; she shall not be moved:
> God shall help her, at the dawn of the morning.
> The nations raged, the kingdoms were moved:
> He uttered his voice, the earth melted.
>
> The Lord of Hosts is with us;
> The God of Jacob is our refuge.

(Psalm 46:1-7 RV – verse 5, margin rendering)

11. The man of sin

In the history of mankind, times of great upheaval and turmoil have often been the opportunity for tyrants to rise to power, or for new ideologies to conquer men with visions of a golden age of equality, justice and freedom. In this century alone there have been a number of such examples. It is interesting to speculate whether Hitler would have gained power in Germany, or Mussolini in Italy, if it had not been for the political and economic turmoil within those lands in the late twenties and early thirties; or likewise whether Marxism would have had the same ability to win the masses of Russia and China, if it had not been for the preceding period of stormy unrest in those countries.

The prophetic word clearly reveals that out of a tumultuous time of shaking, a remarkable and popular leader of the nations would emerge with a new world order. It was John who first called him *the antichrist* when he wrote: 'Dear children, this is the last hour; and as you have heard that the antichrist is coming, even now many antichrists have come. This is how we know it is the last hour' (1 John 2:18). There is no more mysterious figure in the Bible than the antichrist. In its pages he is variously described as *the little horn* (*see* Daniel 7:8, 20, 21, 24, 25; 8:9, 23-25); *the one who causes desolation* (*see* Daniel 9:27; compare Mark 13:14); *the King of the North* (*see* Daniel 11:21-45); *the beast* (Revelation 13:1-18); *the man of sin* (2 Thessalonians 2:3); *the man of perdition* or *the man doomed to destruction* (2 Thessalonians 2:3); and *the lawless one* or *the wicked one* (2 Thessalonians 2:8). In this chapter we shall consider the person of the antichrist as he is revealed in the prophetic word. It is a complex and difficult subject, but it is also a vitally important subject for the people of God, since one of the main features predicted for the end times is his appearance.

Both the vision of the four beasts given to Daniel and the vision of the composite beast given to John allude to conditions of upheaval and change. We should note that the beasts are depicted arising *out of the sea* and in the Bible the sea, which is never still, often symbolizes the unrest and turmoil of the nations. This is particularly emphasized in Daniel's vision: 'In my vision at night I looked, and there before me were the four winds of heaven *churning up the great sea*. Four great beasts .... came up out of the sea' (Daniel 7:2,3, italics mine; compare Revelation 13:1). It was a tempestuous sea out of which the fourth beast arose, 'terrifying and frightening, and very powerful ... and different from all the former beasts'. With it came a little horn with 'eyes like the eyes of a man, and a mouth that spoke boastfully'. This little horn 'will speak against the Most High and oppress his saints and try to change the set times and the laws. The saints will be handed over to him for a time, times and half a time' (*see* Daniel 7:7-8, 25). The same basic features are outlined in John's vision of the beast: 'And I saw a beast coming out of the sea ... The beast was given a mouth to utter proud words and blasphemies and to exercise his authority for forty-two months ... he was given power to make war against the saints and to conquer them. And he was given authority over every tribe, people, language and nation. All the inhabitants of the earth will worship the beast' (*see* Revelation 13:1, 5, 7, 8).

It is clear that both Daniel and John prophesy that in

the last days a leader of unusual talent and power will emerge from a period of unparalleled shaking and tumult. He will lead the world into a new order, promising them wise, authoritative leadership, political and economic stability and strength, and freedom from revolution and the strife of war. Unlike the other world leaders and politicians of the preceding era, who brought government and the democratic system into disrepute by never honouring the promises which they made to their electorates, he will fulfil all his promises to the letter and in a short time create an era free from wars, strikes and terrorism. The nations will be so astonished at the skill and talent of this strong man that they will idolize him to the extent of actual worship.

The universal adulation which he will receive will enable him to introduce an economic system such as the world has never before seen. 'He also forced everyone, small and great, rich and poor, free and slave, to receive a mark on his right hand or on his forehead, so that *no-one could buy or sell unless he had the mark*, which is the name of the beast, or the number of his name' (Revelation 13:16-17, italics mine). In a brilliant stroke of genius he will produce a system in which everyone's livelihood and well-being will be solely in the hands of his administration. It will be a vast 'closed shop' policy, involving the whole of world society from the proletariat to the highest positions in industry, commerce and the professions. He will be able to enforce this system because a strike-weary society, worn out with recessions, uncontrollable inflation and continuous industrial strife, will have willingly surrendered its power to him. For this reason it will not appear to be the form of economic coercion and blackmail which, in reality, it is.

This coming world leader is no ordinary man, for the prophetic word declares that: 'The dragon gave the beast his power and his throne and great authority ... Men worshipped the dragon because he had given authority to the beast, and they also worshipped the beast and asked, 'Who is like the beast? Who can make war against him?' (Revelation 13:2,4). The dragon is identified in the preceding chapter as 'that ancient serpent called the devil or Satan, who leads the whole world astray' (Revelation 12:9). Throughout history Satan has awaited an opportunity to possess totally a man of unique ability and talent. Although there have been a number of men whom he has demonically influenced or inspired, with varying degrees of success, none have fulfilled his expectations. The antichrist will be the first, and the last, to satisfy his ambitions, and for this reason he gives to him his complete support. The devil will give him 'his power and his throne and great authority' in order that he might bring his rebellion against God to a satisfactory conclusion. Satan's plan is to use the antichrist to extinguish the knowledge of God in the earth, to destroy his redeemed people, and to prevent the arrival of God's kingdom by usurping God's authority. His aim is to clear the way to set up an alternative kingdom of his own.

In the history of this age there have been a number of demonically inspired and energized antichrists. John referred to them in the words: '... even now many antichrists have come ...' (1 John 2:18). In recent history one could cite as examples Hitler, Stalin or Mao. This antichrist, however, will eclipse them all. He will not be merely inspired by demons; Satan will enter into him and possess him in the same manner in which he entered Judas Iscariot. It is noteworthy that Jesus described Judas Iscariot as the son of perdition and Paul described the antichrist as the man of perdition (*see* John 13:27; compare John 17:12; 2 Thessalonians 2:3).

It is also clear that some form of worldwide religious authority will give its total support to him. John described another beast which arose out of the earth in the words:

'He had two horns *like a lamb*, but he spoke *like a dragon*. He exercised all the authority of the first beast on his behalf and made the earth and its inhabitants worship the first beast' (Revelation 13:11-12, italics mine). Throughout the book of Revelation the Lord Jesus is called 'the Lamb', and it is an inescapable conclusion that this second beast depicts a false church, and in particular its leadership. In the same way that the first beast depicts the person of the antichrist as well as the politico-economic system which he leads, the second beast also depicts the person of the false prophet and the religious system which he heads. In all likelihood, this false church will be an unholy mixture of the main religions of the world, with 'Christianity' at its base. It has been seriously suggested that the false prophet may be a Muslim, and this suggestion should not be dismissed lightly in view of the Islamic revival and revolution.

The false prophet will perform 'great and miraculous signs, even causing fire to come down from heaven to earth in full view of men' and 'because of the signs ... he deceived the inhabitants of the earth' (Revelation 13:13-14). It has often been the case in history that religion has been the handmaid of tyrannical and evil regimes, providing them with moral justification for their policies. This is certainly the case with the antichrist. The false prophet and the 'church' which he heads, will not only underwrite his policy and conduct, but will also cause the peoples of the world to give their conscience-free allegiance and worship to him.

To understand the real character of the antichrist, the second letter of the apostle Paul to the church at Thessalonica is of vital importance. He wrote the letter mainly to correct some false and dangerous notions among them that the day of the Lord had already arrived. In it he made the emphatic point that it could not come *until the rebellion occurs and the man of lawlessness is revealed*, the man doomed to destruction' (2 Thessalonians 2:3, italics mine). The Greek word translated as 'rebellion' in the NIV, as 'a falling away' in the AV, and as 'apostasy' in the NASB, literally means a defection, a revolt or an apostasy; the last word being the anglicized form of the Greek word.

Paul had already written to them concerning the Lord's coming in his first letter (*see* 1 Thessalonians 4:13-5:11). The amplification of the subject in his second letter is of great practical significance. He wrote that Christians should not be deceived by anyone, since a twofold event had to take place before it would be possible for the day of the Lord to arrive: the rebellion has to occur, and the one who will lead it, the man of sin, has to be revealed.

This rebellion will not be a revolt merely against society's hidebound and outdated concepts and methods, but will be far more serious in its intent. At its heart, it will be a rebellion against God and his law. Its aim is the overthrow of every vestige of the Judeo-Christian ethic and the complete annulment of the influence of God's word in society. This aim will entail the banning of any true preaching of the gospel, Christian teaching and evangelism and, in the end, the liquidation of those who are faithful to the Lord. A false church will be the enthusiastic supporter of this policy, and the result will be a defection from the faith of many lukewarm and self-interested Christians. For this reason it could also be called 'the apostasy'. Daniel described this policy in the words: 'He will speak against the Most High, and oppress his saints and try to change the set times and the laws'; and again: 'The king will do as he pleases. He will exalt and magnify himself above every god and will say unheard-of things against the God of gods. He will be successful until ...' (Daniel 7:25; 11:36). John also wrote in similar vein that: 'the beast ... opened his mouth to blaspheme God and to slander his name and his dwelling place and those who live in heaven' (Revelation 13:6).

John defined the spirit of the antichrist when he wrote: 'It is the man who denies that Jesus is the Christ. Such a man is the antichrist – he denies the Father and the Son': and again: '... every spirit that does not acknowledge Jesus is not from God. This is the spirit of the antichrist, which you have heard is coming and even now is already in the world'; and yet again: 'Many deceivers, who do not acknowledge Jesus Christ as coming in the flesh, have gone out into the world. Any such person is the deceiver and the antichrist' (1 John 2:22; 4:3; 2 John 7). It is clear that the antichrist will be characterized by a hatred of the Lord Jesus, and by a denial of his person and work.

The reason for this vehement antagonism towards the Messiah is not obscure, for the apostle Paul prophesied that: 'He opposes and exalts himself over everything that is called God or is worshipped, and even sets himself up in God's temple, proclaiming himself to be God' (2 Thessalonians 2:4). The antichrist will claim to be God incarnate. In the light of this falsehood, it should be apparent why he is called the *anti*christ, the man of *sin* and the *lawless* one.

It would be impossible to over-emphasize the fact that 'lawlessness' lies at the root of his policy and of the new order which he will introduce. It is not a 'gangsterism' but the refusal to have or to uphold any rule of moral conduct. In the case of his new world order, it will be an official contempt for the law of God in particular, and for all moral law in general. The increasing amorality of modern generations is a preparation for the appearance of the antichrist.

What is the meaning of the apostle Paul's words: 'He ... even sets himself up in God's temple ...'? Some Christians consider the phrase implies that a third temple will be built in Jerusalem and that the antichrist will take it over and make his claim of divinity from it. While it is possible that these words will have such a literal fulfilment, it is questionable whether that is its true meaning. The problems confronting the rebuilding of the temple are vast and complex. For example, the re-institution of a valid priesthood, of a qualified levitical service, and of animal sacrifice on the scale required by the law, present immense problems. They would be difficult to solve without irrevocably dividing Jewry. To these considerable problems, more have to be added. For instance, the fact that the temple site is in Muslim hands and occupied by the Dome of the Rock and the El Aksa Mosque makes the situation even more complex. They could be removed by an act of God, which is entirely possible. It would, however, be impossible to rebuild the temple on the site unless Islam had first received a death blow, or at the least, a crippling blow. A further problem would be the time needed to rebuild it on the scale required, and with the special quality of work and materials its nature demands; it would take a number of years. Even determining the exact position of the various courts and buildings on the site, would take some time before the actual building could begin.

It is possible that these problems could be miraculously overcome in the same manner in which Israel was reborn and Jerusalem was regained. Nevertheless, one has a real sympathy with the Hassidic sect of *Neturei Karta* and some Christians, who place the rebuilding of the temple after the Messiah has come. They believe that he alone could rebuild it, since he is the only one capable of solving the problems connected with its reconstruction.

Furthermore, the theological problems relating to it are not inconsiderable, and should not be lightly dismissed. Many Bible students have real difficulty in believing that a type which has been fulfilled will be followed by its re-institution. For what possible reason, they ask, would the sacrifice of lambs which found its fulfilment in the death of God's Lamb be re-introduced in a rebuilt temple? If it were to be a super-synagogue, with a modern-type priesthood, and without animal sacrifice, it might satisfy some people. But the majority would still be dissatisfied, since in their view the rebuilding of the temple must entail both a priesthood and a sacrificial system according to the law.

It is, however, possible to understand the words of the apostle Paul in a different manner. In all his letters he used the word 'temple' to describe either the church of God, or the bodies of the redeemed, as the dwelling place of God in the spirit (*see* for example 1 Corinthians 3:16-17; 6:19; 2 Corinthians 6:16; Ephesians 2:20-22). If this is true, it follows that his words could be a prediction that the antichrist would substitute a *new kind of worship* for the worship of the Living God, and would outwardly destroy his church by gaining control of it. This will be his policy, whether the temple is rebuilt or not, for whichever view one holds the consequences will be the same. John prophesied: 'men *worshipped* the dragon ... they also *worshipped* the beast ... all the inhabitants of the earth will *worship* the beast.' He also prophesied that the false prophet would make 'all the earth and its inhabitants *worship* the first beast', and he will order 'them to set up an image in honour of the beast...' and, 'he was given power to give breath to the image ... so that it could speak and cause all who refused *to worship* the image to be killed' (Revelation 13:4, 8, 12, 14, 15, italics mine).

These measures will initiate a time of fierce repression and persecution more severe in its nature than anything previously experienced, and the saints will only be delivered from it by a miraculous intervention of God in a rapture of glory. Daniel prophesied of this:

'As I watched, this horn was waging war against the saints and defeating them, until the Ancient of Days came and

pronounced judgment in favour of the saints ... and the time
came when they possessed the kingdom ... The saints will be
handed over to him for a time, times and half a time'; and
again: 'He will cause astounding devastation and will succeed
in whatever he does ... he will destroy many and take his
stand against the Prince of princes. Yet he will be destroyed,
but not by human power'; and yet again: 'There will be a time
of distress such as has not happened from the beginning of
nations until then. But at that time your people – everyone
whose name is found written in the book – will be delivered
... it will be for a time, times and half a time. When the power
of the holy people has been finally broken, all these things
will be completed' (Daniel 7:21-22, 25; 8:24, 25; 12:1,7).

John also testified to this: 'He opened his mouth to
blaspheme God, and to slander his name and his dwelling
place ... He was given power to make war against the
saints and to conquer them' (Revelation 13:6,7).

The Lord Jesus prophesied of this limited period of
severe persecution when he spoke of the 'abomination
which causes desolation standing where it does not
belong' (Mark 13:14; note margin 'he'; compare verses
12,13,15-23; Matthew 24:9-25; Luke 21:10-19). The term
'abomination which causes desolation' first appears in
Daniel chapter 11 verse 31, and chapter 12 verse 11, in
connection with the Seleucid King Antiochus IV
Epiphanes (175-163 B.C.), the archetype of the antichrist
in the Bible. He instituted a reign of terror among God's
people, the worst part of which began in December 167
B.C.. In that month he set up on the brazen altar of the
temple an idol of Zeus, or Jupiter, fashioned in his own
likeness and ordered a daily sacrifice of a pig to be made
on it. His antagonism towards God's people was so bitter
that at its dedication he had the blood of a pig sprinkled in
the holy of holies. At the same time a royal decree was
made ordering all Jews to renounce the law of God and
offer sacrifices to pagan Greek deities. The choice was

stark; it was either a total renunciation of the Living God, or death. this term, therefore, refers in general to the person of antichrist, to his cruel policies and to his armies; and refers in particular, to the evil changes which he makes in the house of God and the ensuing blood bath and desolation. It is interesting to note that Luke substitutes the words 'armies' for 'the abomination which cause desolation' in Luke 21:20-23 (compare Matthew 24:15-21; Mark 13:14-18).

This period of persecution will be the same if the antichrist stands in a rebuilt temple, as both Antiochus IV (167 B.C.) and Titus (A.D. 70) defiled it by their presence and actions, or if he gains control of the church of God and outwardly pollutes and devastates it. Whichever view is held, it will signal the last part of the great tribulation.

Biblical numbers are frequently used in an unbalanced and unhealthy manner. It is, however, noteworthy that in connection with the last phase of world history various figures of times, months and days are given, all of which equal approximately three-and-a-half years. For example, a time, times and half a time (Daniel 7:25; 12:7); forty-two months (Revelation 11:2; 13:5); 1290 days and 1260 days (Daniel 12:11; Revelation 11:3; 12:6). There is also a further figure given of 2300 days, which is approximately seven years (Daniel 8:14).

Are these numbers to be understood literally or are they to be spiritualized? The figure 'a time, times and half a time' could be spiritualized to mean a period of time cut short by the grace of God, being half of seven which is the biblical figure for completeness, fulness or perfection. This interpretation could be extended to cover all these figures, including also the three-and-a-half days in which the dead bodies of the two witnesses will lie in the streets of Jerusalem (see Revelation 11:9,11). Nevertheless, one questions the reason for precise figures being given for days and months if they are not literal. If these figures are accepted literally, however, another problem arises: it should be possible, once this time of tribulation has begun, to fix a date for the coming of the day of the Lord. On this matter, the Lord Jesus expressly stated that; 'No-one knows about that day or hour, not even the angels in heaven, nor the Son, but only the Father. Be on guard! Be alert! You do not know when that time will come' (Mark 13:32-33). For Christians who are unable to believe in a rapture of the saints before, or during the tribulation, this problem has to remain unsolved.

A question which has vexed Christians and been the cause of heated debate over the last century, is whether or not the redeemed will escape the great tribulation. The subject has been made more complex by the multitude of interpretations and explanations, some of which should receive a prize for their sheer versatility in mental acrobatics and contortions.

In my view, one fact emerges clearly: the saints, a term only applied in Old and New Testaments to those saved and set apart by God's grace, are to be found in that time. It is impossible to study the relevant passages in the prophetic word with an open mind, and deny that fact. Even if Daniel's references to 'the saints' are dismissed by some interpreters as relating only to the Jewish people (*see* for example Daniel 7:21,25; 11:24-25; 12:1), it is not so easy to dismiss John's prophecy: 'He was given power to make war against the saints and to conquer them' (Revelation 13:7). Similarly, it would be difficult to ignore the fact that Paul was writing to Christians when he warned: 'Don't let anyone deceive you in any way, for that day will not come until the rebellion occurs, and the man of lawlessness is revealed ...' (Thessalonians 2:3; compare verses 1-2). Furthermore our Lord's words concerning this period plainly refer to the presence of his disciples in it (*see* Mark 13:9-23; Matthew 24:9-28). Are these saints those who have been saved after the church

has been raptured? In my view, it is an unwarranted
conclusion for it has to be based on an 'implication' rather
than the plain meaning of the relevant Scriptures.

Daniel prophesied that the antichrist 'will become very
strong, *but not by his own power*' (Daniel 8:24, italics
mine). Paul amplified this when he wrote:

> 'The coming of the lawless one will be in *accordance with the
> work of Satan* displayed in all kinds of counterfeit miracles,
> signs and wonders, and in every sort of evil that deceives
> those who are perishing' (2 Thessalonians 2:9-10, italics
> mine). It is a salutary lesson that miracles, signs and wonders
> are not the infallible sign of God's presence and working.
> Satan is also able to perform them. During the last days, the
> people of God will need an unusual measure of spiritual
> discernment because the false prophet and his co-workers
> will perform such signs and miracles that, if it were possible,
> the elect could be deceived' (*see* Matthew 24:24).

Daniel also prophesied that the antichrist 'will be
destroyed, but not by human power' (Daniel 8:25). It
should be a source of practical encouragement for those
who know the Lord that he is called 'the man of
perdition', or 'the man doomed to destruction'. Daniel
was told that 'the court will sit, and his power will be taken
away and completely destroyed forever'. In a later vision
he was again told: 'Yet he will come to his end, and no-one
will help him' (Daniel 7:26 11:45). His rise to power, the
time he will remain in power and his end are alone
determined by God. God holds him back until the proper
time for him to be revealed has come; the antichrist is
unable to extend his rule by one day more than fore-
ordained; and when his appointed time has arrived, the
Lord Jesus will slay him with the breath of his mouth, and

bring him to an end by the appearance of his coming (*see* 2 Thessalonians 2:3,6,7).

There have been a number of explanations concerning the means which God uses to restrain the secret power of lawlessness and the appearance of the lawless one (*see* 2 Thessalonians 2:7,8). In my view, whatever it is that constitutes the restraint, whether it is the work of the Holy Spirit, the presence in the world of a functioning church, human government or divinely ordained angelic ministry upholding law and order in society, the lawless one is unable to be revealed until God commands its withdrawal. Both his coming and his destruction are fore-ordained.

I have already made a number of references to Antiochus IV Epiphanes, for he figures prominently in the vision given to Daniel (*see* Daniel 8:9-14, 23-25; 11:21-45). He reigned for only eleven years (175-163 B.C.) but his reign was destined to become one of the most traumatic eras in Jewish history. In the Bible he is *the* archetype of the antichrist, and from his character, his rule and his policies, it is possible to learn much concerning the one he prefigures. He took the name Epiphanes which means 'outshining'. As a name it could mean 'Illustrious', but in his case it meant 'God manifest', since he believed that he was the manifestation of a god, probably Zeus or Jupiter. In spite of that he was not a fanatically religious man but a fervent believer in Hellenic culture and civilization.

He was born in Athens, and at one point in his life was made the chief magistrate of the city and a master of the Mint. He remained so popular with its citizens that they made him an honorary citizen. Although the prophetic word rightly describes him as 'a contemptible person' and 'a stern-faced king, a master of intrigue' (*see* Daniel 8:23), from the world's point of view he was very different from that description. He was a highly cultured, sophisticated and intelligent man of vision, firmly believing in the form of democracy which was at that time practised in the Greek city states. He was a good soldier and administrator; a strong man with strong, clear policies, which, if necessary, he was prepared to expedite ruthlessly.

Although born in Athens, and receiving a Greek education, which was to leave him enamoured of Greek culture and ways all his life, he was in fact a Greek-speaking Syrian of Macedonian origin. He became king of the Seleucid empire in 175 B.C.. His domain centred on Syria, but included Babylonia, and part of Asia Minor and Greece. The Ptolemaic Empire, centred on Egypt, was its arch rival for territory and power, and the two were intermittently at war for their whole history. The Holy Land was strategic to both of them, being situated between their territories. At the time when Antiochus IV came to the Seleucid throne the Holy Land belonged to the Seleucids.

His vision was to unite the nations of the eastern Mediterranean basin in a pan-Hellenic 'common market', in which the economic causes of strife, revolution and war would be removed. In all probability he saw it as a first stage in the regaining of the vast empire, which Alexander the Great had won a century and a quarter earlier, but which by then had broken up into warring factions. The keynote of his policy was 'unity', which he saw in terms of an economic, cultural and moral unity. He foresaw the necessity to overcome cultural, linguistic and religious differences which were additional causes of war and strife. His policy, therefore, was to impose Greek culture, thought and customs upon the peoples of his domains, and to make Greek the official language. Since the Greek attitude to religion and morality was liberal, he foresaw no problem in making it the basis of his religious policy.

In the non-Jewish world he was popular and his policies were considered to be progressive. Many Jews also co-operated fully with his policies, believing that his

Hellenism was enlightened. It was the faithful Jews who were the one obstacle to his complete success. The more faithful they were to 'their' God's law, the more exclusive and unyielding they appeared. They lived differently, dressed differently, kept special dietary laws, observed special days and worshipped an unseen God. There was nothing attractive about them in the eyes of Antiochus. They appeared to him to be no more than narrow-minded, bigoted and anti-progressive fanatics. Having first sought in every way to gain their co-operation and having failed, Antiochus decided to use force. It was the beginning of a nightmare period of testing for the faithful.

It began quietly with changes in various laws and the introduction of new laws, which made it difficult to remain uncompromised. It progressed until it reached the last three-and-a-half years in which it was virtually impossible to remain alive and not compromise. Those years began with Antiochus taking over the temple, changing its worship and service, and defiling it. In 167 B.C. circumcision, Sabbath observance and the reading of the Bible were forbidden by royal decree; immoral rites were performed in the temple; faithful Jews were forced to eat non-kosher foods, especially pork. In December of that year an idol to Zeus, which I have previously mentioned, was erected in the temple, and the land ran with the blood of the faithful. The end came in 164 B.C. not with the success of Antiochus and his vision but with the victory of the Jewish Maccabbees and the purpose of God.

Certain characteristics of the antichrist emerge from this portrait of Antiochus IV. He will be a cultured, sophisticated, clever man, a man of supreme vision for the future of the world. His policies will appear logical, enlightened and progressive, with a twofold aim of banning war and terrorism and producing stability and prosperity. His watchword will be unity; unity in every sphere of life whether economic, cultural, social, racial or religious. He will be acclaimed a saviour and deliverer by a war-weary world, exhausted with its economic, social and racial problems.

Only in regard to his religious policies will his real character emerge, for he will be dedicated to the destruction of the word of God, and the Judeo-Christian heritage. He will identify true believers as narrow-minded, reactionary fanatics, obstructing the path of progress, and undermining the people's unity. He will use every means available to persuade them to forsake their 'bigoted and exclusive faith', join a 'world church', and participate in the new order and system. When these means fail, his savagery will be unbounded and he will seek to liquidate them. Nevertheless in spite of his worldwide prestige and influence and the fact that his authority and policies will appear unchallengeable, the monolithic system, which he heads, will be overthrown in a moment of time by the coming of the Lord Jesus. 'Then the sovereignty, power and greatness of the kingdoms under the whole heaven will be handed over to the saints, the people of the Most High. His kingdom will be an everlasting kingdom, and all rulers will worship and obey him. This is the end of the matter' (Daniel 7:27-28). The rule of the antichrist is only for a short itme; the kingdom of God and his Messiah is for ever.

12. The coming of the Son of Man

The climax of all history, as revealed in the prophetic word, is the coming of the Messiah. The whole Bible is sharply focused upon that single event as the divine and practical solution to the world's inherent problems. Like a great symphony the Bible moves towards its final movement in which its many themes find their complete expression and fulfilment. In his return all the glorious purposes of God find their practical realization.

The work of Calvary is incomplete without his second coming. It is the logical and concluding act in a sequence of events which began with the creation and the fall of man, progressed to the Messiah's coming at Bethlehem, his atoning death, and his all-powerful resurrection and ascension. It is an interesting fact that the prophets of the Old Covenant saw both the first and the second coming of the Messiah as a continuous whole. They saw his birth, his death and his kingdom and glory, as an unfolding sequence without any long intermissions.

The coming of the Messiah is *the* event to which all biblical prophecy points. Indeed the Bible's most dramatic and vivid imagery is used in relation to his majestic return. Jesus spoke far more concerning his coming again than he spoke of either his cross, or the church. That is a noteworthy point which devalues neither of those truths, but emphasizes how vital it is to both of them.

His second coming is also the ultimate crisis of human

history, both inescapable and irreversible. It is neither a slow evolutionary process of betterment, nor a mystical, vague and 'spiritual' experience. It is a sudden, public and literal intervention of God in the course of world history, by which he will terminate the old fallen disorder with its emptiness, strife, injustice and misery, and introduce his kingdom. Consider, for example, some of the phrases used in connection with his return: 'For the Lord himself will come down from heaven, with a loud command, with the voice of the archangel and with the trumpet call of God ...'; 'in a flash, in the twinkling of an eye, at the last trumpet. For the trumpet will sound ...'; '... when the Lord Jesus is revealed from heaven in blazing fire with his powerful angels ...'; '... and every eye will see him ...' (1 Thessalonians 4:16; 1 Corinthians 15:52; 2 Thessalonians 1:7; Revelation 1:7).

There is a simple, direct and dogmatic clarity in the manner in which the word of prophecy proclaims the return of the Messiah. Many of the details surrounding it have been open to debate and even controversy. On the fact of his actual return, however, it is not possible to be either vague or hazy, providing one fully accepts the authority of God's word. For example, the statement made by the angels to the disciples on the Mount of Olives is neither vague nor abstract but specific: the Lord Jesus will personally return in the same manner in which he ascended. ' "Men of Galilee," they said, "Why do you stand here looking into the sky? This same Jesus, who has been taken from you into heaven, will come back in the same way you have seen him go into heaven" ' (Acts 1:11). It would be difficult to find a more specific statement than this one. Even a child in their company could have understood the plain and obvious meaning of their words: Jesus will literally return.

For the same reason it would be impossible to misconstrue the words of the Lord Jesus: 'At that time the sign of the Son of Man will appear in the sky, and all the nations of the earth will mourn. They will see the Son of Man coming on the clouds of the sky, with power and great glory' (Matthew 24:30); or to misinterpret his words before the Sanhedrin, 'And you will see the Son of Man sitting at the right hand of the Mighty One and coming on the clouds of heaven' (Mark 14:62). It is obvious that he meant his words to be taken literally.

Space would not permit me to quote all the statements of the apostles concerning the second coming of the Lord Jesus, for they are too numerous. The early church proclaimed it with a dogmatic certainty. For example, Paul wrote to Titus: 'while we wait for the blessed hope – the glorious appearing of our great God and Saviour, Jesus Christ ...' (Titus 2:13). John also prophesied; 'Look, he is coming with the clouds, and every eye will see him, even those who pierced him, and all the peoples of the earth will mourn because of him. So shall it be! Amen' (Revelation 1:7). Peter, preaching to the multitude in Solomon's porches, also stated the same truth: ' .... that he may send the Christ, who has been appointed for you – even Jesus. He must remain in heaven until the time comes for God to restore everything, as he promised long ago through his holy prophets' (Acts 3:20-21). From these and many other such statements, it is clear that the apostles and the early church believed in a literal coming again of the Lord Jesus.

In a similar vein, Daniel prophesied in a clear and plain manner concerning the Messiah's coming when he said:

'In my vision at night I looked, and there before me was one like a son of man, coming with the clouds of heaven. He approached the Ancient of Days and was led into his presence. He was given authority, glory and sovereign power; all people, nations and men of every language worshipped him. His dominion is an everlasting dominion that will not pass away, and his kingdom is one that will never be destroyed' (Daniel 7:13-14).

Zechariah is even more specific when he prophesied: 'Then the Lord will go out and fight against those nations … On that day his feet will stand on the Mount of Olives, east of Jerusalem … The Lord will be king over the whole earth. On that day there will be one Lord, and his name the only name' (Zechariah 14:3,4,9).

There is no way in which it is possible for any of these prophecies to be 'spiritualized' into a vague prediction of an impersonal 'messianic' golden age, without mishandling the word of God and distorting its true meaning. They are concise and plain statements of truth. It would be more honest to reject them totally than to 'spiritualize' them in such a manner that their real significance is destroyed. It is clear that the Bible in general, and the New Testament in particular, proclaims the literal and personal return of the Messiah, Jesus. Moreover, it proclaims it in terms of unmistakeable clarity and childlike simplicity. It would be difficult to accept the Bible as the authoritative and inspired word of God and deny that fact. Faithful Christians of all generations and persuasions are one in this belief, and affirm it in the simple words of the creed '… from whence he shall return to judge the quick and the dead'.

Let us consider certain aspects of his second advent on which all Christians are agreed in principle. His return will be the final vindication by God of all that is true and of himself. It will provide the conclusive proof that Jesus is the Messiah, the Son of the Living God, and the Lamb of God who bore away the sin of the world; that salvation is to be found in no one else since there has been no other name under heaven given to men through which it is possible to be saved. It will be the absolute vindication of the person, the work and the words of the Lord Jesus.

It will also be the vindication of all those who have truly followed him regardless of the cost. The joy that was set before him, which enabled him to endure the cross, will be the joy into which all those who belong to him will enter at his coming. He will present them before his glorious presence without fault and with great joy. Then the redeemed will enter Zion with singing, their mouths filled with laughter, and their tongues with songs of joy; everlasting joy will crown their heads (*see* Jude 24: Isaiah 35:10; Psalm 126:2).

The word of God will be vindicated at the second advent of the Messiah, for it will then be proved to have been thoroughly reliable, accurate and relevant. It will be clear that it was not foolish to have trusted his word and obeyed him, even though at times it had appeared to be the height of foolishness. For however we identify those people who will be ashamed at his coming, it will not be those who have put their whole trust in him and his word. In that day it will be transparently clear that their afflictions were 'light and momentary' when compared with the weight of eternal glory which those troubles had produced in them.

Furthermore, his coming will finally prove that only when God is king will the universe be right and in harmony. The Messiah will be the practical solution to all the problems of this world, whether they are political, economic, ecological, ethnic, social or moral. The prophetic word has difficulty in describing the effect on the whole creation of his coming and reign. John prophesied of it, saying:

> 'Then I saw a new heaven and a new earth ... And I heard a loud voice from the throne saying, "Now the dwelling of God is with men, and he will live with them ... he will wipe every tear from their eyes. There will be no more death or mourning or crying or pain, for the old order of things has

passed away." He who was seated on the throne said, "I am making everything new!" ' (Revelation 21:1, 3-5).

The apostle Paul adds to our understanding of this matter when he wrote:

'I consider that our present sufferings are not worth comparing with the glory that will be revealed in us. The creation waits in eager expectation for the sons of God to be revealed. For the creation was subjected to frustration, not by its own choice, but by the will of the one who subjected it, in hope that the creation itself will be liberated from its bondage to decay and brought into the glorious freedom of the children of God. We know that the whole creation has been groaning as in the pains of childbirth right up to the present time. Not only so, but we ourselves, who have the firstfruits of the Spirit, groan inwardly as we wait eagerly for our adoption as sons, the redemption of our bodies' (Romans 8:18-23).

The prospect of a creation liberated from its bondage to decay and free to become what God intended it to be fills one with wonder and amazement. If while subject to corruption it is so beautiful, what will it be when the Messiah releases it? It is a prospect of glory which our minds and hearts are not able fully to comprehend. Isaiah described the effect of this liberation when he prophesied:

'The wolf will live with the lamb, the leopard will lie down with the goat, the calf and the lion and the yearling together; and a little child will lead them. The cow will feed with the bear, their young will lie down together, and the lion will eat straw like the ox. The infant will play near the hole of the cobra, and the young child put his hand into the viper's nest. They will neither harm nor destroy on all my holy mountain, for the earth will be full of the knowledge of the Lord as the waters cover the sea. In that day the Root of Jesse will stand as a banner for the peoples; the nations will rally to him, and his place of rest will be glorious' (Isaiah 11:6-10).

Isaiah's description of the natural creation is very different from the 'nature red in tooth and claw' with which we are acquainted. He paints a picture of a paradise which has eluded man since before the deluge. The key to this radical change is the presence of the Messiah, and the prophecy begins with the promise that 'a shoot will come up from the stump of Jesse' and predicts that 'with righteousness he will judge the needy, with justice he will give decisions ... Righteousness will be his belt, and faithfulness the sash around his waist' (Isaiah 11:1,4,5).

So deeply moving is this prospect that the prophets speak of the mountains and hills 'bursting into song' and the trees of the field 'clapping their hands', and the trees of the forest 'singing for joy'! For example, Isaiah cries: 'You will go out in joy, and be led forth in peace; the mountains and the hills will burst into song before you, and all the trees of the field will clap their hands. Instead of the thornbush will grow the pine tree, instead of briars the myrtle will grow. This will be for the Lord's renown, for an everlasting sign, which will not be destroyed' (Isaiah 55:12-13). And in a similar vein the Psalmist declares: 'Let the heavens rejoice, let the earth be glad, let the sea resound, and all that is in it, let the fields be jubilant, and everything in them. Then all the trees of the forest will sing for joy; they will sing before the Lord, for he comes, he comes to judge the earth. He will judge the world in righteousness and the peoples in his truth' (Psalm 96:11-13).

It is hard to imagine a world in which absolute truth, absolute righteousness and absolute love are the foundation for all government. This world has become hardened to compromise and co-existence with evil and injustice as a realistic and justified policy. It has become accustomed to murderers being entertained in lavish style; being embraced by other heads of state and given banquets at which pleasant, fulsome and untrue tributes are made to them on the basis of diplomacy. It is difficult to conceive of a world in which this would not only be unnecessary but unthinkable, a world in which the conduct and policies of government would be based on truth and not on compromise, on righteousness and not on the need of co-existence with evil. Yet of the Messiah it is said: 'a king will reign in righteousness' and 'a king who will reign wisely and do what is just and right ...' and 'In your majesty ride forth victoriously on behalf of truth, humility and righteousness ... Your throne, O God, will last for ever and ever; a sceptre of justice will be the sceptre of your kingdom. You love righteousness and hate wickedness ...' (Isaiah 32:1; Jeremiah 23:5; Psalm 45:4,6-7).

'When the Son of Man comes in his glory, and all the angels with him, he will sit on his throne in heavenly glory. All the nations will be gathered before him, and he will separate the people one from another as a shepherd separates the sheep from the goats' (Matthew 25:31-32). When he returns, he will set right all the wrongs not only of contemporary world society, but also of history, for 'he is the one whom God appointed as judge of the living and the dead' (Acts 10:42; compare 2 Timothy 4:1; 1 Peter 4:5). Jesus declared: 'The Father judges no-one, but has entrusted all judgement to the Son ... And he has given him authority to judge because he is the Son of Man' (John 5:22,27). And Paul said: 'For he has set a day when he will judge the world with justice by the man he has appointed' (Acts 17:31). John more fully describes the final judgement in the words; 'Then I saw a great white throne and him who was seated on it ... And I saw the dead, great and small, standing before the throne, and books were opened. Another book was opened, which is the book of life. The dead were judged according to what they had done as recorded in the books ...' (Revelation 20:11-12). No evil or wrong, however cleverly concealed, or deviously 'planted' at the time on innocent parties, will remain unexposed. All will be brought to the light, and the Lord Jesus will arbitrate and judge in every matter.

Even a cup of water given to one of his disciples will not be overlooked (*see* Mark 9:41; compare Matthew 25:31-46).

Everyone and everything will be judged by him, except those who have been saved through his finished work. He has already paid the penalty of their sin, when he bore its judgement in his body on the tree. The apostle Paul stated this truth when he wrote:'God made him who had no sin to be sin for us, so that in him we might become the righteousness of God'. He also wrote to the Roman Christians: 'Therefore, there is now no condemnation for those who are in Christ Jesus' (2 Corinthians 5:21; Romans 8:1). Those who have been born of God will not face him as their judge but as their redeemer. Nevertheless they will appear before his judgement seat to give account of themselves and their stewardship, as it is written: 'For we must all appear before the judgement seat of Christ, that each one of us may receive what is due to him for the things done while in the body, whether good or bad'; and 'So then, each of us will give account of himself to God' (2 Corinthians 5:10; Romans 14:12; compare Romans 14:10-11; 1 Peter 4:5; 1 Corinthians 3:10-15). This will mean either his commendation and reward, or his disapproval and loss, a loss not of salvation but of status in his eternal government and kingdom.

The righteousness and holiness of God is the source of his determination to judge all things. Divine truthfulness requires justice to be done as regards the whole history of man, and that, in turn, necessitates judgement. If any individual, whether great or small, could outwit or deceive him, and thus escape judgement, it would raise grave doubts about the character of his rule and kingdom. It will not be possible and John records: 'The sea gave up the dead that were in it, and death and Hades gave up the dead that were in them and each person was judged according to what he had done ... If anyone's name was not found written in the book of life he was thrown into the lake of fire' (Revelation 20:13,15). On the deepest level, it is his love and compassion for those who have been wronged, which demands justice finally to be done.

On these truths related to the second advent there is general agreement among Christians at least in principle, if not in detail. But will all these events come to pass immediately at his coming? We must now face the vexed question of the millennium. Is there a thousand year reign of the Messiah between his second coming and the general resurrection of the dead, the final judgement, and the new heaven and new earth, or will his coming introduce the ages of eternity? This subject has been the basis for much heated debate and controversy, and not a few divisions. The word 'millennium' which means 'a thousand years' is taken from Revelation chapter 20 verses 1-7, where it occurs six times. Opponents of the view are quick to point out that it is the only occasion in the Bible where it occurs, and that all the numbers in the book of Revelation are symbolic.

Nevertheless, it is not possible to dismiss it so easily. For instance, how are we to explain the presence of sin, evil, disease, of birth, and death in many prophecies which plainly refer to the time after the Messiah's return (see for example Isaiah 65:17-25; Zechariah 14:1-5,9,16-21; Revelation 21:17; 22:2,15)? The problem becomes more complex when we recognize the fact that the devil will have been 'thrown into the lake of burning sulphur' and with him all who perpetrate evil (see Revelation 20:10,14,15;21:8). Furthemore in eternity there will be no more marriage, birth or death (see for example Matthew 22:30; Revelation 21:4). To explain these many prophecies as poetic licence is unacceptable since it would reflect seriously on the honour of God, and weaken faith in the accuracy of his word. The vision which John records in Revelation chapter 20 has also to be satisfactorily expounded. To interpret the thousand years as either the church age which began at Pentecost, or a period within it, leaves much to be desired. How is the reference to the first resurrection to be explained and, in particular, the words. 'The rest of the dead did not come to life until the thousand years were ended' (Revelation 20:5; compare verses 4,6). It was a fashionable view amongst many Christians in the eighteenth and nineteenth centuries that the world was slowly becoming christianized through the preaching of the Gospel, and gave rise to support for such interpretations. The twentieth century has tended to undermine confidence in them.

In my view Revelation chapter 20 is part of a series of consecutive events given to John in vision form: the destruction of Babylon (Revelation 18); the marriage supper of the Lamb (Revelation 19:1-10); the battle of Armageddon and the end of the antichrist and the false prophet (Revelation 19:11-21); the thousand year reign of the Messiah in which Satan is bound, to be set free for a short time at its end (Revelation 20:1-10); the general resurrection and the final judgement (Revelation 20:11-15).

It is my belief that there will be a millennium. It would not alter my faith or joy in the Lord, if there were no such period. I find myself unable to hold such a conviction in an argumentative or hotly dogmatic spirit. If we are honest, both views present us with problems which are not easily answered. The vital need is to be ready for the Lord's coming and for all that will follow it. Nevertheless, for the reasons already stated, it seems to me that the prophetic word predicts a glorious earthly Messianic kingdom in the world as we know it, over which the Messiah Jesus will reign. It will be a seventh and Messianic day, as opposed to the six days of fallen man's history.

There is further reason for believing in a millennium. In my estimation, it is the final vindication of God and of his Messiah before the nations. God will prove, through the millennial reign of the Lord Jesus, the truth of his word. It will be the time for the restitution of all things which was spoken of by the apostle Peter (see Acts 3:21). God will also prove that even with the reign of the Prince of Peace, with his righteous, just and compassionate government, worldwide peace and prosperity, the reversal of decay and the healing of disease, *there is no alternative to being born of God*. Once the devil is released the nations follow him in violent rebellion against God. There remains in them the ground of deception. Thus God will finally prove that no superficial, 'cosmetic' answer will solve man's deep-seated problems. Only a new birth, with a change of origin and nature, will suffice. As John wrote: 'The reason the Son of God appeared was to destroy the devil's work. No-one who is born of God will continue to sin, because God's seed remains in him; he cannot go on sinning, because he has been born of God' (1 John 3:8-9). It is a salutary lesson that people are not necessarily changed or saved by clear-cut evidence of God's truth. Even when confronted with the presence of the risen and glorified Messiah and his saints, and the many miracles of the millennial reign, they will still not come to the salvation of God.

The words of the apostle Paul will also be fulfilled during this time: 'Then the end will come, when he hands over the kingdom to God the Father after he has destroyed all dominion, authority and power. For he must reign until he has put all his enemies under his feet ... When he has done this, then the Son himself will be made subject to him who put everthing under him, so that God may be all in all' (1 Corinthians 15:24-25,28).

Whether we believe there will be a millennium or not, the second advent of the Messiah will lead to a new heaven and a new earth, the home of righteousness, to a new Jerusalem, the bride and wife of the Lamb, coming down out of heaven, irradiating the glory of God. It will be an earth filled with the knowledge of the glory of the Lord, as the waters cover the sea; an earth in which swords will have been beaten into ploughshares and spears into pruning hooks; where nation will not take up sword against nation, nor train for war any more; a world in which the law will go out of Zion, and the word of the Lord from Jerusalem (see 2 Peter 3:13; Revelation 21:9,10; Habakkuk 2:14; Isaiah 2:3-4). The end will be the same, whether everything will be introduced at his coming, or some things will await the conclusion of his thousand year reign; God will be all in all.

13. So you also must be ready

Whatever view is held concerning the coming of the Lord, the great need is to be ready for his appearing. It is not possible to substitute anything else for readiness and alertness. Mere knowledge of the complex details of the second advent without the resulting preparation of heart and mind will only bring the greater condemnation. The Lord Jesus underlined this need in the words: 'Therefore keep watch, because you do not know on what day your Lord will come .... So you also must be ready because the Son of Man will come at an hour when you do not expect him' (Matthew 24:42,44). It is sad that this subject has become a battlefield of conflicting views, at times betraying an unchristlike spirit in the protagonists. Instead of the truth effectively challenging and influencing the people of God to be ready for his appearing, more interest is often shown in establishing the rightness of a particular view.

It will be impossible to be prepared for the return of the Lord Jesus if the Holy Spirit has not been allowed to settle the many issues in the life of the believer. Sometimes those issues appear so trivial that one could dismiss them as totally insignificant. Yet often a universe of new spiritual life, power and discovery depends on an act of trusting obedience to the Lord. Such faith and obedience are the essential constituents of discipleship. Furthermore, to be his disciple entails discipline and training. The

Spirit of truth himself is in charge of that education and he is faithful and firm in his dealings with a disciple. The cost of discipleship is always high, for the truth has to enter our inner being and perform its work. If, however, we would serve the Lord and our fellow-believers, it is necessary to be liberated from any bondage to self and the world by such a growing, practical knowledge of the truth.

A readiness for his return will also involve us in taking up our cross, giving up all right to ourselves, and following him the whole way. If we are to be prepared, there is no possibility of escaping the challenge of his cross. It will mean nothing less than the laying down of our lives for him, and this will prove too costly and difficult unless our real treasure is in the Lord Jesus. Only then will our hearts be in the right place. To reveal the unfathomable riches of the Messiah to believers is the Holy Spirit's work and he alone can enable them to experience that spiritual fullness in practical and trying circumstances.

An experience of the anointing of the Holy Spirit is another essential in a genuine preparation and readiness of heart for his coming. There will be no way to overcome in the situations and difficulties of the last days without the person of the Holy Spirit. We need to be immersed in him, experiencing his fullness and power, otherwise we shall fall asleep, or be sidetracked. Furthermore, he alone is able to keep us alert and sensitive to the movements of the unseen. To be ready for the appearing of the Lord implies an understanding of the times in which we live. The Holy Spirit is able to give that understanding through the word of prophecy, while at the same time preserving us from the possibilities of excess and imbalance. If we pay little or no attention to that word shining like a lamp in a dark place, we condemn ourselves to stumbling around in the dark without either understanding or direction. As we proceed to consider the return of the Messiah in greater detail, it is important to bear in mind this paramount need to be ready for his appearing. All else is secondary.

Will his return be one event or movement, or is it preceded by a rapture of the saints? The subject is exceedingly complex although to hear or read the dogmatic proponents of the different views, one would think that it was a simple matter. When with an open mind, however, all the relevant scriptures are brought together, the difficulties become apparent. It is clear that the Lord Jesus foresaw the diversity of view which would arise on this vital matter, and could have resolved the problem by giving a short discourse setting out in unmistakable clarity the sequence of events surrounding his return. The fact that he gave no such summary is significant and certainly not accidental. The manner, therefore, in which he spoke of it must be by design, for *he said enough to enable believers to be prepared and ready*, and not enough to allow them to walk by sight rather than by faith. He intends our reliance in the last days to be on him through the person of the Holy Spirit, rather than in the false security engendered by the knowledge of a catalogued programme of events.

The most simple way of approaching his second advent, in the eyes of many, is to view it as one movement. The church of God will go through the great tribulation until he comes gloriously to deliver her. In that tribulation period many will be purified and many will fall away. When his people are caught up to meet him in the air, they will immediately accompany him on his return. The proponents of this view often state that 'there are not two second comings but one'! It has an attractive simplicity about it, and the added advantage that it was the view of the church fathers and the reformers. Nevertheless when the relevant scriptures are explored in depth, a number of problems appear.

For instance, the Lord Jesus repeatedly warned that we

will not know the time, the day or the hour of his coming
(*see* for example Mark 13:32-33; Matthew 24:36,42,44;
25:13; Luke 12:40). When, however, the sign of the Son of
Man appears in the sky, the timing of his return will be
obvious. Apparently this sign will appear sufficiently in
advance of his coming to cause widespread apprehension
and mourning (*see* Matthew 24:30; compare Luke 21:25-
27). To answer this objection by stating that the believer is
not meant to know the day or the hour but is expected to
recognize the year of his appearing is contrary to the
Lord's many specific warnings. It has led to more than a
few tragedies. The followers of the Lamb are meant to
recognize the general period of the end. But his solemn
prediction that his coming would be unexpected by even
his closest disciples, has to be taken seriously. It was to
Peter, Andrew, James and John, representing those
disciples who were the most devoted and responsible in
his work, that he said: 'So you also must be ready, because
the Son of Man *will* come at an hour when you do not
expect him.' He did not say because the Son of Man *may*
come at an hour when you do not expect him (Matthew
24:44, italics mine; compare Mark 13:3).

Another noteworthy point is that throughout his discourse in Matthew 24, from verses 4 to 28, the Lord Jesus
refers directly to his people as 'you'. This indicates their
presence on the earth in the events he predicts. From
verse 30, however, there is an abrupt and unexplained
change to '*they* will see the Son of Man ...' (compare also
Mark 13:5-23 with verse 26; Luke 21:8-20 with verse 27).
It would seem that his disciples are no longer present on
earth.

Similarly, if believers are to pass through the great
tribulation, witnessing the advent of the antichrist and the
false prophet, and experiencing worldwide persecution,
they should be able to date the coming of the Lord
reasonably accurately. Even if the great tribulation lasts

more than seven years, it should be possible to time its conclusion by the incidents predicted for it in prophecy. Once that is a feasibility, the dating of the time of the Lord's return to within one or two years becomes possible. This is in conflict with the whole tenor of our Lord's clear warnings.

The Lord Jesus declared that: 'two men will be in the field; one will be taken and the other left ... Therefore keep watch, because you do not know on what day your Lord will come. But understand this: if the owner of the house had known at what time of night the thief was coming, he would have kept watch ...' (Matthew 24:40-43). It has been long observed that there are two sides to the Messiah's return. On the one hand, it is described as a public and dramatic coming – his sign appearing in the sky as a herald; with blazing fire, trumpets sounding, and a loud voice of command; with every eye seeing him and reacting to his appearing. On the other hand, it is described as a secret, hidden coming, like a thief in the night – quiet, stealthy, unexpected and sudden (see for example Luke 12:39-40; 1 Thessalonians 5:2,4; Revelation 16:15). It is noteworthy that the Messiah used both descriptions in the major discourse on his return.

Is it the same event which is described in these different ways? The words of the apostle Peter would seem to support the view that it is. He said: 'But the day of the Lord will come like a thief. The heavens will disappear with a roar; the elements will be destroyed by fire ...' (2 Peter 3:10). He makes no mention of a secret rapture of the saints. Nevertheless, it is significant that in both Matthew 24:40-44 and 1 Thessalonians 4:13-5:11, the reference to their being taken up is followed by the warning that his coming for them would be like that of a thief. In the light of the confusion that has arisen over the subject, it is hard to understand why such diametrically opposed descriptions were used if it were the same event.

These problems gave rise to another view of the second advent which has become a widely held view in evangelical circles during the last two centuries. It began with many of the leading teachers of the Christian Brethren in the early eighteenth century and received an immense impetus during the Second Evangelical Awakening of the mid-nineteenth century. Basically it differentiates between the coming of the Lord *for* his saints and the coming of the Lord *with* his saints. It considers the rapture, Christ's coming for his own, to be a distinct event destined to take place before the great tribulation. In the rapture all who are born of God, whether faithful or unfaithful, will be caught up to be with the Lord, and will be preserved by the grace of God from the horrors of the great tribulation.

Adherents of both interpretations are agreed that not only those who have died in Christ, but those who are alive at his coming will accompany the Lord on his return (*see* for example Matthew 24:30-31,40-41; Mark 13:26-27; Luke 21:27-28; 17:34-35; 1 Thessalonians 4:13-18; 3:13; 2 Thessalonians 2:1; Zechariah 14:1-5; compare Jude 14-15; Revelation 19:11-21). It is the distinction made between the rapture of the saints and the coming of the Lord which is the point of disagreement.

In my estimation, the prophetic word places a far greater emphasis upon the rapture than some interpreters would allow. A plain reading of the relevant scriptures would not suggest that it was merely a taking up of the saints in order that they might return immediately with him. For instance, it is interesting to note that the marriage supper of the Lamb, recorded by John in Revelation, is followed by a description of the Messiah leading the armies of the saints to the battle of Armageddon. His return is apparently preceded by the marriage supper (*see* Revelation 19:11-21; Zechariah 14:1-15; compare Revelation 19:1-10; Ephesians 5:25-

27). If the Lord Jesus is to present the bride to himself as a 'radiant church', and enjoy the marriage supper with her, the raptured saints could not immediately return with him. There must be a lapse of time between the two events.

Consider also the Messiah's reference to his coming 'as a thief'. He declared: 'Behold I come like a thief! Blessed is he who stays awake and keeps his clothes with him, so that he may not go naked and be shamefully exposed' (Revelation 16:15; compare verses 12-16). What possible meaning has this statement in the context of the Armageddon battle? By the onset of that war the nearness of the Messiah's return should be obvious to all believers, even those who have a minimal spiritual understanding and insight. Furthermore, there could be no more public display than when he rides forth form heaven on a white horse to that battle as the Word of God, as King of kings and Lord of lords. There is nothing about his coming on that occasion which is like that of a thief (*see* Revelation 19:11-16)! If, however, it is a reference to a sudden and hidden coming of the Lord to take his own beforehand, its significance is clear. It is a gracious word of warning and encouragement to those who belong to him to be ready.

If all the relevant scriptures and their implications are taken into consideration, it is not so easy to dismiss this view of his coming. An oft-repeated objection to it is that it is more complex than the first view. That is undoubtedly true, but a matter is not necessarily false or erroneous because it is complex. A more serious objection is centred in the words of the Lord Jesus; 'At that time men will see the Son of Man coming in clouds with great power and glory. And he will send his angels and gather his elect from the four winds, from the ends of the earth to the ends of the heavens' (Mark 13:26-27; see also Matthew 24:30-31). His words would not suggest a rapture *before* his coming but *at* his coming. Similarly, another objection is that the apostle Paul dogmatically stated that believers would not be 'gathered to him' ...'until the rebellion occurs and the man of sin is revealed'. This clearly suggests that the people of God must enter into at least part of the great tribulation, and accords with a clear statement by the Messiah himself (*see* 2 Thessalonians 2:1-3; Mark 13:11-24).

A third view of the second advent also emerged during the last two centuries but never became so widely held. Some of the most outstanding and able Bible teachers of that period, hower, were among its exponents, including D.M. Panton, G.H. Pember and G.H. Lang. It grew, in part, out of a dissatisfaction with the two earlier views, neither of which, it was considered, represented the whole truth concerning the Lord's coming.

This interpretation also considers the rapture to be a distinct event that will take place before his return, but not necessarily before the beginning of the great tribulation. Its proponents have given various times for it either before or during the first half of that period. The unique feature of this view is its belief that only those Christians who are faithful to the Lord and walking with him, will be raptured. The rest will pass through the tribulation and be purified by it. For this reason it has been called 'the partial rapture' or 'the selective rapture'.

The view is founded on an important truth concerning the overcomers, or the overcoming remnant, which is drawn from all parts of God's word and not only from prophetic scriptures. The scope of this book would not allow me to do full justice to it, but it is not possible to dismiss the teaching easily. Its view of the rapture is based, in part, upon the Lord's warnings to his disciples that he would come for them unexpectedly, like a thief. It is considered that these repeated warnings, given either by direct word, or in parable form, indicate that he will take only those who are sufficiently prepared.

It sees two kinds of 'church' being present in the last days, the Philadelphian and the Laodicean. To his faithful ones in the Philadelphian church, he says: 'Since you have kept my command to endure patiently, I will also keep you from the hour of trial that is going to come upon the whole world to test those who live on the earth. I am coming soon. Hold on to what you have, so that no-one will take your crown. Him who overcomes I will make a pillar in the temple of my God. Never again will he leave it. I will write on him the name of my God, and the name of the city of my God, the new Jerusalem ... I will also write on him my new name' (Revelation 3:10-12). But to unfaithful, self-satisfied and worldly Christians, he says:'I know your deeds, that you are neither cold nor hot. I wish you were either one or the other! So, because you are lukewarm – neither hot nor cold – I am about to spit you out of my mouth ... to him who overcomes, I will give the right to sit with me on my throne ...' (Revelation 3:15-16, 21). The former believers he will rapture because they are ready; the latter he will make either hot or cold through tribulation.

The vision given to John and recorded in Revelation chapter 12 is considered to be a crucial revelation concerning the overcomer and the rapture. According to this view the woman represents the church and the man-child, who is caught up to God and his throne, represents the overcomers. The problem in it is the statement:

'Then the dragon was enraged at the woman and went off to make war against *the rest of her offspring – those who obey God's commandments and hold to the testimony of Jesus*' (Revelation 12:17, italics mine).

Some identify 'the rest of her offspring' as those believers who will pass through the tribulation and become overcomers during its course. But if 'the woman' is the church, and she is given a place of safety in the earth, 'out of the serpent's reach', it is hard to understand how her more faithful offspring are within his reach (*see* Revelation 12:13-17).

This interpretation of the second coming is generally linked to a special view of the millennium. It holds that only the overcomers, those who have grown to a certain spiritual maturity in the Lord through discipline and suffering, will be raised in the first resurrection. The rest of the dead in Christ will await the final resurrection. At the rapture, the overcomers from among the dead in Christ will be joined by the overcomers among the living and will at some point shortly afterwards return with the Messiah to reign with him for a thousand years. These are the saints who have been conformed fully to the likeness of the Lord Jesus and who have been trained in 'kingship' through the things they have suffered. They will constitute the Messianic administration for both the millennium and the eternal ages to come. They are not an elite company to whom God had given special advantages and privileges, but those of his children who have fully appropriated and exploited the potential in his grace and salvation. In fact, they are basically an advance working party, giving to the Lord their supreme devotion, securing the fulfilment of his purpose, and clearing the way for the rest of his people ultimately to follow them.

The apostle Paul made a most arresting statement in the testimony he gave, when he wrote: 'and so, somehow, to *attain* to the resurrection *from* the dead' (Philippians 3:11; italics mine). Since the resurrection of the saints is a work of God's grace and part of their salvation, what is meant by the use of the word 'attain'? Furthermore, the phrase translated 'from the dead' is also remarkable. It is literally translated 'the out-resurrection from among the dead'. Was Paul referring to a special resurrection of the overcomer, a resurrection of those who would be part of the bride of the Lamb and would reign with him? He proceeded to declare: 'Not that I have already obtained all this, or have already been made perfect, but I press on to *take hold of that for which Christ Jesus took hold of me* ... One thing I do ... I press on *toward the goal to win the prize* for which God has called me heavenward in Christ Jesus' (Philippians 3:12-14, italics mine). There is another mysterious scripture which may also refer to the same kind of resurrection. It is written of certain saints under the old covenant: 'others were tortured and refused to be released, so that they might *gain a better* resurrection' (Hebrews 11:35, italics mine).

This interpretation of the second advent certainly answers most of the objections to the other views. It explains simply the Lord's insistent warnings on the need to be ready, since the rapture would be a sudden and unexpected event, only including those who were faithful and prepared. It would also explain his words: 'Be always on the watch, and pray that you may be able to stand before the Son of Man' (Luke 21:36). If every one born of God is included in the rapture, one wonders why he instructed us to pray that we might escape all that would happen and stand in his presence? Similarly, if all believers are to pass through the tribulation, what are we to escape? However, if only those who are faithful to the Lord will be taken, the need to seek him for grace and power is self-explanatory.

The objections to this view have been many and often heatedly expressed. Many times it has been stated that it creates more problems than it solves. In my view, that is not true. If the whole prophetic word is taken into consideration, it presents us with the least problems. Nevertheless, it is not problem-free.

A common charge made against it is that it teaches 'elitism'. If there are some Christians who claim that *they* are 'overcomers', and are numbered among the Lord's elite, it is a clear indication that they are not! The objection itself, however, is weak. The Lord has a perfect right to take to himself 'firstfruits', since he is able to recognize those who have ripened before the rest of the harvest is gathered.

Furthermore, it is impossible suddenly to confer on saints the *ability* to govern, unless there has been a previous maturing of spiritual character, and a whole-hearted submission to his disciplined training. Through sin, unbelief or apathy, some of us are unable to govern ourselves, our homes, our work, the 'kitchen sink', or even the dog, let alone participate in his eternal adminis-tration. For this reason there are many warnings in God's word that although we will not lose our salvation, it is possible to lose our place in his throne and in his government (*see* for example Romans 8:17; Philippians 3:10-14; 2 Timothy 2:12; Revelation 3:21; 1 Corinthians 9:24-27).

Another charge against it is that it teaches 'rapture or reward by works' and not 'salvation by grace'. This objection is also weak, for the word of God clearly warns believers that they will suffer loss if they refuse to press on with the Lord. It is not their works which obtain the reward or the crown, or enable them to sit down with the Lamb in His throne. It is the grace of God in them which has been fully exploited by each individual believer.

There are, however, more serious objections than these. One is the fact that a plain reading of the prophetic word would not immediately suggest a partial rapture. For example, in his words relating to his coming for his own, the Messiah could have made the matter clear by saying: 'one of *you* will be taken and the other left' instead of the more general 'one will be taken, and the other left' (*see* Matthew 24:40-41; Luke 17:34-35). Similarly, in the apostle's description of the rapture there is not the faintest suggestion that only the faithful among his own will be raptured. In fact, his words give the impression that all those who are born of God will be included (see 1 Thessalonians 4:13-18).

Furthermore, if the bride consists only of the overcomers and the marriage supper of the Lamb takes place between the rapture and his coming, who are those blessed ones who are invited to it? They are obviously not the bride, since it is in her honour that the marriage feast is being given. Are they the angels, or the saved in glory who did 'not overcome? If they are neither of these, it necessitates making two categories of overcomers, the bride and those invited to the wedding. Some have, in fact, made this distinction between overcomers.

If only the overcomers from among the living and the dead participate with the Messiah in the millennium, what happens to those believers who survived the last part of the tribulation and will be alive at the Lord's coming? Will they all be overcomers as a result of the tribulation? If they are, they will have missed the wedding feast and marriage. On the other hand, if they are saved but not all overcomers, what will be their position in the millennium?

This brief consideration of the three major schools of thought concerning the Lord's return has not been stated in a mocking or argumentative spirit. I have sought to make clear the fact that whichever view is held, there are problems relating to it. All these views and the variations on them present the honest Bible student with difficulties which are not easily explained. Many of my readers will hold either one or other of them, and will have answered the objections to it to their own satisfaction and peace of mind. However, it is good to remember that aggressive dogmatism on detail in such a complex subject as the second advent is rarely healthy. When it is made an excuse for division or faction, it has become an evil. There are major truths in God's word on which God's people are entitled to be, and indeed should be dogmatic. There are also areas of detail relating to major truths which are not sufficiently clear to allow such dogmatism. On those details it is good to hold honest convictions, while at the same time remaining open-minded, and maintaining fellowship with those who see them differently. At the risk of repeating myself, one fact needs to be underlined. The Lord Jesus could have made this matter absolutely clear by one short discourse in which he outlined the sequence of events. That this was not so was by design. Instead of giving us a clear-cut and catalogued programme, he calls on us to be ready for him whenever he appears.

The truth on which there *can* be unanimous and dogmatic clarity is the literal and glorious return to this earth of the Lord Jesus as King of kings and Lord of lords. On that day his pierced feet will stand again upon the Mount of Olives in Jerusalem, and peace and joy will come at last to this war-torn and weary world. On that day, his redeemed will be with him in glory with bodies like his. The out-standing truth for the believer is that, whenever he comes to take his own people to himself, on that day they will be with him. The word which the mouth of the Lord has spoken will have come to pass: 'And the glory of the Lord shall be revealed, and all flesh shall see it together' (Isaiah 40:5).

14. Watch

'What I say to you, I say to everyone: "Watch!" ' That was the pungent and challenging manner in which the Lord Jesus concluded his major discourse on his coming recorded in the New Testament (Mark 13:37). He had commenced it in similar vein: 'Watch out that no-one deceives you …' (verse 5; 'take heed' AV; RV). It is both arresting and instructive that whenever the Messiah refers to his return and the events of the last days, he repeatedly warns his desciples to watch, to be on their guard, and to be ready (*see* Matthew 24:4,42-44; 25:13; Mark 13:5,9,23,33,37; Luke 12:37-40; 21:8,34-36). In whatever manner these phrases are translated into English, they are all associated in thought. They reveal an underlying theme in everything he said concernig the end times; *the paramount need is to be awake and prepared*. There is nothing in his words which is conducive to complacency or carelessness with regard to those days.

It is no small paradox that the very teaching which was given to challenge us to be awake and alert has sometimes been used to breed a complacency in believers. They consider that it is unnecessary to take any action to be prepared because they are saved and 'will not be there on the earth' when the predicted events take place. This is not the work of the Holy Spirit, but the work of an enemy. At the very least, we need to be ready for his coming, even if there is no great tribulation for the redeemed to pass through and endure. What kind of bride is it, we may ask, who could be careless about the attitude of her heart towards her bridegroom, about her looks and her dress, as her wedding day approaches? No serious and well-informed student of the Bible could dogmatically declare that the Lord's people will not suffer in the days which lie ahead before the rapture, or that there will be no war, disasters, serious privations or persecutions, through which they will have to pass before he appears for them. What kind of arrogance or superiority could make Western believers conclude that *they* will never have to face what their fellow believers behind the Iron and Bamboo curtains have already faced in this generation?

Even so, the charge is sometimes made that any emphasis on this kind of truth, or even the mention of it, only spreads fear amongst the people of God. In my view, it would be infinitely better to spend a few sleepless nights over the issue, and spiritually awaken, than to sleep until it is too late. No one will ever thank a servant of God for gently rocking God's people to sleep when they should have been challenged to be his disciples, and to endure hardness as good soldiers of the Lord Jesus Christ.

It is time to hear the words of the Lord Jesus: 'What I say to you, I say to everyone: "Watch!" ' If he repeatedly warned us to be prayerful, on our guard and ready, there must be some possibility of spiritual loss, if his call is ignored. It is possible that when those events predicted by the Lord Jesus begin to be fulfilled, complacent and unprepared Christians could lose their faith and collapse. It is therefore high time to awake and prepare ourselves.

Are we, however, merely to watch for our own good and security, or has the Lord also laid a responsibility for others upon our shoulders? It is clear beyond dispute that both the church and the child of God have a solemn and divinely given responsibility for which the Lord holds them accountable. Long ago, the Lord spoke to Ezekiel and defined the responsibility of a watchman:

'Son of man, I have made you a watchman for the house of Israel; so hear the word I speak and give them warning from me. When I say to a wicked man, You will surely die, and you do not warn him or speak out to dissuade him from his evil ways in order to save his life, that wicked man will die for his sin, and *I will hold you accountable for his blood*. But if you do warn the wicked man and he does not turn from his wickedness or from his evil ways, he will die for his sin; but you will have saved yourself' (Ezekiel 3:17-19; italics mine).

Ezekiel might have been a watchman over only his own spiritual growth and well-being, but God had made him responsible also for a nation. The Lord made this matter even more clear in the words:

'The word of the Lord came to me: Son of man, speak to your countrymen and say to them: "When I bring a sword against a land and the people of the land choose one of their men and make him their watchman, and he sees the sword coming against the land and blows the trumpet to warn the people, then if anyone hears the trumpet but does not take warning and the sword comes and takes his life, his blood will be on his own head. Since he heard the sound of the trumpet but did not take warning, his blood will be on his own head. If he had taken warning, he would have saved himself. But if the watchman *sees the sword coming and does not blow the trumpet to warn the people* and the sword comes and takes the life of one of them, that man will be taken away because of his sin, but *I will hold the watchman accountable for his blood*" ' (Ezekiel 33:1-6; italics mine).

It is not possible to have a living and saving relationship with the Lord, to be his disciple, and have no responsibilities other than for one's own spiritual growth and well-being. Inherent in our salvation is a responsibility for the world around us. It is obnoxious to God when his people withdraw into a pious circle of believers, separated from the world in every way, with a concern only of their own blessing, satisfaction and fulfilment. When the church of God shows no concern for the world and its lost destiny, it reveals a spiritual heartlessness which cannot please the Lord. It is criminal to be silent and uncaring when the people of God, above all other peoples, know what will happen to this world and to the unsaved.

Isaiah prophesied: 'I have posted watchmen on your walls, O Jerusalem; they will never be silent day or night. You who call on the Lord, give yourselves no rest, and give him no rest till he establishes Jerusalem and makes her the praise of the earth' (Isaiah 62:7-7). Those who are born of the Spirit and are spiritually growing up are watchmen whom the Lord has posted on the walls of Jerusalem. The duties of a city watchman are to guard the interests of the king and of the city at all times, but especially at night. The Lord has posted watchmen upon 'the walls of Jerusalem' that they might spiritually guard the interests of his name and kingdom. They are there to watch and pray. True intercession is essential if the work of God is to be established and reach his desired end. Such prayer warfare is linked to being spiritually alive and watchful, otherwise the watchmen themselves could be deceived by enemy devices and be overtaken by disaster.

Sometimes one hears the opinion voiced that prayer of this kind is unnecessary, since in any event the Lord will fulfil his purpose. It is, however, a fallacy. Although the Lord is able to fulfil his whole purpose without our prayer, he has chosen to involve us in its outworking for our education and training. It is with an eternal vocation in mind that he has enlisted us. A fatalistic approach to the events of the last days is, therefore, as dangerous as ignorance or complacency. The divine call is into a fellowship with the Lord in intercession in order that the complete fulfilment of his purpose may be secured. Genuine intercession is fellowship in action. The head, the Lord Jesus, is *the* intercessor. The body, his church, are intercessors with him, working under his direction, travailing with his burdens and triumphing through his anointing. When seen in this light, prayer warfare is vital if the plans of the Lord are to be fulfilled in the last days.

In ancient times the watchman spotted the movements of both friend and foe long before anyone else was aware of them, and took the necessary action. The supreme qualification of a watchman is the ability to see clearly, otherwise he would be incompetent and virtually useless. As we move into all the conflict and pressure of the last days, this ministry of watchfulness will become even more important. It is a costly ministry, for whilst others sleep the watchman must remain awake until daybreak. If he falls asleep with the rest, the people of God may be enslaved and compromised, or at the least, robbed and spoiled. His priority is to guard the interests of the Lord at all times, and especially through the night.

The duties of a city watchman are also to blow the trumpet and sound the alarm when he becomes aware of danger, so that the rest of the people may take action and be ready. There is only one company of people in the world qualified to proclaim God's truth to the nations, and warn them of things to come. It is the community of God's redeemed people, the church of the Lord Jesus. She alone has a God-given understanding of coming events and of the ultimate divine goal to which everything is heading. To no other people has God entrusted the word of prophecy. She is designed to be that vessel or instrument through which the Lord is able to communicate with the nations, expressing his heart and mind, sharing his saving love and mercy, and warning of coming judgement, whether general or particular. If the church is silent, who else can communicate the truth to the world? Who else can blow the trumpet, or sound the alarm? Who will warn the world of what is coming upon it, or hold forth the word of life to any who would truly seek God? If the church fails in her responsibility in this matter, the door is left wide open to the domain of false cults and sects, to the blind leaders of the blind. It is also left open to those eccentric and unbalanced Christians who by their pronouncements and antics bring the prophetic word into such disrepute. If we are moving inevitably and irreversibly into the last days, a solemn responsibility rests upon all who belong to the redeemed family of God.

The Lord Jesus said, 'You are the salt of the earth ... You are the light of the world. A city on a hill cannot be hidden ... In the same way, *let* your light shine before men, that they may see your good deeds and praise your Father in heaven' (Matthew 5:13,14,16; italics mine). The true church of God is intended to be a 'prophetic community'. She is called not only to preach the prophetic word to the world, but to reveal by her life and conduct that she also believes it. She is the salt of the earth which is intended to halt corruption and infection in society. She is not meant to face society with the fatalistic attitude that the darkness and evil in it are unchallengeable. By her presence in the world, by spiritual authority, prayer and action, she is designed to check wickedness in it. She is the light of the world which is able to pierce the thickest darkness, reveal the truth about conditions and light up the path which has to be trod. She is a city built on a hill which is obvious to all. The truth in action is there for all to see.

In the revelation of John there is a striking and mysterious statement: '... I am a fellow-servant with you and with your brothers who hold to the testimony of Jesus. *Worship God! For the testimony of Jesus is the spirit of prophecy*' (Revelation 19:10, italics mine). It should be noted that the phrase 'the testimony of Jesus' is found throughout the book of Revelation and is always associated with the word of God, as if the two matters are complementary (*see* Revelation 1:2,9; 6:9; 20:4). The testimony of Jesus is not merely what he proclaimed, tremendous as that is, but also what he revealed in and through himself. He is 'the heart of God revealed'. It is this testimony of Jesus which the church holds. She is like a lampstand holding the lamp with its light.

The apostle Paul stated it simply: 'God has chosen to make known among the Gentiles the glorious riches of this mystery, which is Christ in you, the hope of glory' (Colossians 1:27). This is not meant to be a marvellous yet impractical thought; it has vital relationship to the church of God expressed on the earth. It is certainly not a question of mere church pattern, function or method of church life and government. It is possible to be correct in all of that, and yet the lampstand has been removed (*see* Revelation 2:5). The 'thing' rumbles on but the heart of the matter has gone.

The testimony of Jesus is related to himself as head expressing himself through many members. Together, as head and body, they express and communicate the mind and heart of God to both the seen and unseen world. The ability of the head to direct his members is vitally important, if the body of Christ is to grow and function in any place. Anything which severs the head from the body, or even comes between them, however scriptural it may seem, will result in the lampstand being withdrawn. It is not enough, therefore, to bear witness to the word of God, or even to keep his commandments; there has to be also the experience of the living Messiah as head of his church. As head he must be owned, sought, heard and obeyed. It is for this reason that the Lord emphasizes the necessity for first love. Only that quality of love is able to ensure that this relationship to him is guarded above all else (*see* Revelation 2:3,5).

Wherever the testimony of Jesus is being held by a company of God's people, the spirit of prophecy is present. The fellowship of his children becomes prophetic in itself. It becomes a revelation, a manifestation and a declaration of its head and Saviour in the place in which it lives. Being bound together in his fellowship, they become the means by which others see the love, the mercy and the glory of God, and experience his salvation. They are constituted a prophetic vessel, to communicate the word of prophecy to people who walk in darkness and dwell in the land of the shadow of death. If the Holy Spirit who has inspired that word is in the midst of such a people, then he will take the Bible and will make it live again to others. It is not merely what they preach but what they are. The word of Christ has come to *dwell* in them richly; the *implanted* word has taken root, is growing up and is bearing fruit (*see* Colossians 3:16; James 1:21). They become the place where God meets man and man meets God. Those who seek the truth will gain understanding among them; they will receive the key to human history, to what is happening and what will happen in the world, to the meaning of life and to the divine goal of all. In the growing darkness of the days in which we live, this is the calling of God's people.

However unpalatable the truth may appear, a night is coming which will cover the whole earth. It will be an 'hour of darkness' in which the forces of evil will have a terrible but shortlived triumph. It is this which constitutes the urgent need for God's people to be prepared. Beyond that night, there is coming a morning which nothing in heaven or hell can stop. It is God's day and until it dawns the prophetic word is powerful, valid and relevant for us. Even when it predicts and outlines dark and evil matters, it is the day of the Lord on which it focuses all attention.

It causes to pass before our gaze all those symbols of the night – the dragon, the beast, the false prophet, the harlot and Babylon with all her splendour and wickedness. In their heyday they appear supreme and invincible; even eternal. But they have a beginning and an end; not one of them is eternal. They all belong to the night which is passing away. How much of that night the people of God will have to pass through is open to question. What we know with certainty is that the Lord will not fail his own, but will provide them with all that is necessary to overcome and to sit down with him on his throne. For those who belong to God belong to a new day; the sun of righteousness has already risen for them with healing in its wings. They are sons of the light and sons of the day and belong to neither night, nor darkness. They are God's city, the new Jerusalem, in which there is no night. Although they live in a world of darkness it is not their home; their faces are turned toward his daybreak (*see* Malachi 4:2; 1 Thessalonians 5:5; Revelation 21:25).

The night passes but the day of the Lord is for ever. From Genesis to Revelation the word of prophecy looks towards the dawning of that day and the glory of the Lamb whose reign is eternal. It never fastens our attention on the dark events of the night, but directs our gaze to the Lord's day and the glory that will be. Even when the end is near, it proclaims: 'when these things begin to take place, *stand up and lift up your heads*, because your redemption is drawing near' (Luke 21:28, italics mine).

So certain is the Lord's word that he commands us to *worship him* in the midst of all these troubles. The posture of *'standing with head lifted up'* is the Jewish form of worship. We have no need to fear when those events which he has predicted begin to be fulfilled. We have only cause to worship, for our redemption is drawing near.

To such followers of the Lamb, Peter wrote: '… we have the prophetic word made more sure, to which you do well to pay attention as to a lamp shining in a dark place, until the day dawns, and the morning star arises in your hearts' (2 Peter 1:19 NASB). Till the day dawns, the word of the prophecy has been entrusted to us.

Battle for Israel

by Lance Lambert

Israel — not just for the tourist.
It's a geographical knot in a tug of war between the
super powers.

This book takes you into the political as well as
the spiritual conflict.
Written by a man with inside information.
He presents a perspective not to be found
anywhere else.

Lance Lambert, long time friend of prominent
Israeli leaders and an authority on the Bible history
of the Israeli nation, is the author. He gives an 'on
the scene' account of the Yom Kippur War — he
predicts the future — his insight is unique.

Never before has one man been allowed to enter
into the confidence of Israelis to such an extent —
Lambert, a Christian, welcomed and loved by
Jews, describes the Battle for Israel.

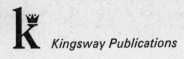
Kingsway Publications

The Uniqueness of Israel

by Lance Lambert

Woven into the fabric of Jewish existence there is an undeniable uniqueness. Israel's terrain, her history and chief city, all owe their uniqueness to the fact that God's appointed Saviour for the world was born a Jew. His destiny and theirs are for ever intertwined.

There is bitter controversy over the subject of Israel, but time itself will establish the truth about this nation's place in God's plan. For Lance Lambert, the Lord Jesus is the key that unlocks Jewish history. He is the key not only to their fall, but also to their restoration. For in spite of the fact that they rejected him, he has not rejected them.

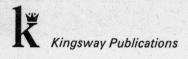

Kingsway Publications